Telling Silence

SUNY series, Insinuations: Philosophy, Psychoanalysis, Literature
───────────
Charles Shepherdson, editor

Telling Silence

Thresholds to No Where in Ordinary Experiences

CHARLES E. SCOTT

Cover photo: "Enjoy the Silence . . ." by Thomas Leuthard. CC BY 4.0.

Poetry extracts from *The Selected Poetry of Robinson Jeffers* used with permission. "Why I Wake Early" by Mary Oliver. Reprinted by the permission of The Charlotte Sheedy Literary Agency as agent for the author. Copyright © 2004, 2005, 2014, 2017 by Mary Oliver with permission of Bill Reichblum.

Published by State University of New York Press, Albany

© 2023 State University of New York

All rights reserved

Printed in the United States of America

No part of this book may be used or reproduced in any manner whatsoever without written permission. No part of this book may be stored in a retrieval system or transmitted in any form or by any means including electronic, electrostatic, magnetic tape, mechanical, photocopying, recording, or otherwise without the prior permission in writing of the publisher.

For information, contact State University of New York Press, Albany, NY
www.sunypress.edu

Library of Congress Cataloging-in-Publication Data

Name: Scott, Charles E., author.
Title: Telling silence thresholds to no where in ordinary experiences / Charles E. Scott.
Description: Albany : State University of New York Press, [2023] | Series: SUNY series, Insinuations: Philosophy, Psychoanalysis, Literature | Includes bibliographical references and index.
Identifiers: ISBN 9781438495194 (hardcover : alk. paper) | ISBN 9781438495200 (ebook) | ISBN 9781438495187 (pbk. : alk. paper)
Further information is available at the Library of Congress.

10 9 8 7 6 5 4 3 2 1

Contents

Acknowledgments — vii

Introduction — 1

Fragment One: Intimations: Telling Silence — 11

Fragment Two: The Vastness of the Sensuous — 13

Fragment Three: Connie's Walk in the Forest — 15

Fragment Four: A Silent Gap's Power — 17

Fragment Five: Being True to Nothing — 20

Fragment Six: Haunting Silence — 22

Fragment Seven: Dwelling with Silence — 26

Fragment Eight: "That Silence" — 29

Fragment Nine: Interpreting Silence? Deviations and Interruptions in Hermeneutics in the Lineages of Zeus's Messenger — 31

Fragment Ten: Interpreting in Discontinuities — 37

Fragment Eleven: Silence, Really? — 41

Fragment Twelve: Sensibilities with Silences — 43

Fragment Thirteen: Discovery in Darkness and Light — 45

Fragment Fourteen: Sense of Silence — 48

Fragment Fifteen: Sudden Sparks and Wonders of My Solitude: Silent Creation and Free Spirits — 57

Fragment Sixteen: Breaches of Divisions — 66

Fragment Seventeen: Silent Space — 81

Fragment Eighteen: Touching Silence — 88

Fragment Nineteen: Moments — 97

Fragment Twenty: A Story of Silent Unreason: Nomadic Freedom with Imagination's Dangerous Instability — 105

Fragment Twenty-One: Spring — 116

Fragment Twenty-Two: The Fall of the Power of Fell Time: Abstractions Treated as Unimagined Realities — 118

Fragment Twenty-Three: A Story about Two Lovers in Pervading Silence Silencing — 124

References — 131

Index — 133

Acknowledgments

I have been fortunate to have insightful people who played a significant part in my writing *Telling Silence*. Kindness, generosity, patience, and exceptional intelligence come to mind as I acknowledge them.

Five people constituted "The Border Thought Workshop," Omar Rivera, Daniela Vallega-Neu, Alejandro Vallega, Nancy Tuana, and I. We met two times during the period I wrote the book, and each time I received helpful critique and stimulation. These sessions in which we read and responded to each other's work-in-progress combined rigor and goodwill that made working together constructive, compatible, and at times exhausting.

David Ferrell Krell read an early version of the manuscript. Many of his comments, text references, and suggestions are woven into the fragments. They made the book better than it would have been without the influence of his gentle and brilliant spirit. Michael Naas gave me invaluable insight in the content and formation of Fragment Twenty-Two. Stephen Swoyer pointed out two references that I integrated into later parts of the book.

Charles Shepherdson, as editor of "Insinuations," a book series for SUNY Press, encouraged and supported my applying to the Press. I was fortunate to have Rebecca Colesworthy for my senior acquisitions editor. Her kindness combined with what I perceived as a musician's sense for tone, rhythm, timing, and exactness of wording made working together a privilege. Céline Parent, my copyeditor, Susan Geraghty, production editor, Matthew John Phillips, indexer, Aimee Harrison, the member of the production department who managed the design of the book cover, and Julia Cosacchi, assistant manuscript editor composed a skilled team—working with them was a pleasure.

Nancy Tuana, my constant companion and most severe critic, is a necessary condition for this book's publication. She made many, many constructive suggestions, questioned wording that I thought was clear (and it wasn't), and, as my interlocutor, allowed me to explore what I wanted to say in various sections and was not quite saying it. Deep gratitude accompanies love, uncanny love, in my acknowledgment of her support.

My thanks to Stanford University Press for permission to reprint Robinson Jeffers, "The Treasure," from *The Selected Poems of Robinson Jeffers*, Stanford, California: Stanford University Press, 2001.

"Why I Wake Early" by Mary Oliver.
Reprinted by the permission of The Charlotte Sheedy Literary Agency as agent for the author.
Copyright © 2004, 2005, 2014, 2017 by Mary Oliver with permission of Bill Reichblum.

Earlier and significantly revised versions of some of the material in Fragments Nine, Ten, Eleven, and Twelve appeared in "Interpreting Silence?," *Research in Phenomenology*, 50 (2020), pp. 1–16. My thanks to the editors of *Research in Phenomenology* for permission to incorporate revised versions of ideas I first tried out in this piece.

Introduction

Why did I write this book? It does not have a religious orientation or a meditative discipline to offer. It is not about rituals that aim to lift us up to a spiritual heaven. It is not primarily a scholarly book about what other people have said about silence. I want, rather, to speak of silence, often indirectly and in such ways as to let silence happen in our awareness undisturbed by objectification. I want to create poietic occasions whereby people might become more aware of silence pervading their lives and the world around them.

Why would I want to do that? People, including me most particularly, are able to become so stuck in the activities . . . the sounds and substances around us that we are not able to notice silence that accompanies activities, sounds, and substances . . . silence throughout the noise of a group of people at a party, silence with a wind blowing through trees, silence in our busy minds, silence of time. We can feel heavy, weighted with distractions, unaware of the ways attunements to silence can open us to dimensions of our lives that, although silence does nothing, can free us from the power of everyday affective bondages and boundaries. A friend of mine, when she felt overwhelmed with everything she *must* do now, would say, "there are too many things . . . just *too many things*!" No time to notice the silence in her life.

Attunements to silence often lighten the burden of those too many things, release the silent bonds that tie us down when our brains seem to be constantly busy with internal dialogues, with songs that frolic in our minds, unrelieved worries and anxieties, responsibilities, deadlines, games, debts, news, calls on our phones . . . always thinking of something or having something on our minds. I want to show that silence pervades spaces of sounds, permeates our bodies and the bodies and relations around us. It suffuses the earth and the sky. Silence is so much a part of our lives that we are insensitive to it and insensitive to our insensitivity to it. I want to speak in such ways that what I call *telling silence* can happen *in* your and my awareness and that our awareness of silence can happen *in* silence as distinct to awareness about silence.

Awareness is an especially important word in this book, one about which I will have much more to say. Here I note that *awareness* as I use the word is immediate.[1] It happens unreflectively, not conceptually. Immediate awareness does not deliberate or ponder. It is neither objective nor subjective, and I will often use the middle voice formation, silence silencing, when I am speaking of immediate awareness in silence.[2]

This book encourages people to become *attuned* with silence in their lives and environments. I repeat for emphasis, it encourages us to become aware of silence *in* silence.[3] I want to show that our lives and lives around us are porous in their happenings, often rather more diaphanous than dense in the pervasiveness of silence and in the absence of uninterrupted presence. I want to show that silence is not a thing, that our lives and our environments are infused with silence, and that awareness of it allows people to be attuned with themselves in their world, attuned with being alive in the insubstantiality of our experiences and the fragility that invests even the strengths of living beings inclusive of other than human lives.

◆ ◆ ◆

A Short Excursus on the Word *Telling*

Telling in the sense I am using the word means affective disclosing, a revealing effect. *Telling* in this book has the connotation of *affective* and stresses an immediate, non-reflective disclosure. A telling occurrence is not necessarily peripheral in a given situation; it can touch in the heart of the matter. I will return often in the early fragments to the meaning of "telling" in connection with silence and awareness in silence.

---

1. I will speak of immediate awareness throughout the book. See "A Short Excursus About Immediate Awareness" in Fragment Fifteen for an extended discussion of it.

2. See the seventeenth fragment for an extended discussion of the middle voice.

3. In the course of the next several fragments I will elaborate the meaning of this phrase, awareness of silence *in* silence.

I structured this book by the use of fragments in my effort to "tell" of silence in a way that lets silence "tell" of itself.[4] Fragment One, Fragment Two, and so forth. The book is fragmented in the sense that it has no continuing narrative that brings all the fragments together, no organized system of concepts with an architecture or an argument that defines the book as a whole. Although there are many stories in the book, the connections among them and among the fragments do not take the form of a continuous narrative. Indeed, were this book written as a carefully structured narrative, it—the book—would mislead readers and lose a sense for telling . . . for effectively disclosive . . . silence. The inclination to connect claims and subtopics logically like a strong argument, or to create a well-conceived system of concepts, or to build a set of ideas that is designed a bit like a well-laid-out city's grid or a formal garden would make alertness to silence in its non-objectivity extremely difficult, if not impossible. Silence tells no stories. It "tells" of itself without narration. Silence "tells" itself with not a thing there to tell. So *what* I say, as what I say silently fades out *in* the telling, is often less important than what I don't say, can't say directly. The telling can happen when some poetic words, images, metaphors, intuitions, and their indirections clear an opening for the disclosure of silence silencing. My hope is that such indirections will encourage an intensified mindfulness of silence *in* silence.

"Indirections," I said, that I hope "will encourage an intensified mindfulness of silence *in* silence." *Poietic* thinking or poietic philosophy are the words that best describe this book's approach in carrying out that hope. The approach has two primary emphases: poietic creation and silence silencing.

First, poietic creation. *Poiein* in Ancient Greek means *to make*. Its connotation suggests activities that bring into being something that did not previously exist and that will persist in unpredictable ways; one could speak of poietic activities that make—affect—differences in feelings with uncertain futures. Or one might say that an action resulted in certain

---

4. The fragments are part of this book's poietic style about which I will say more. Philosophers like Jacques Derrida, Martin Heidegger, Søren Kierkegaard, and Friedrich Nietzsche use fragments to suit their particular purposes. I have my own purposes that were generated as I worked on awareness of silence and that are quite different from those of my respected predecessors.

effects.⁵ Poietic language and thought in this book function with creative interplays of imaginative, intuitive, and conceptual formations. The boundaries that poietic activities form are dynamic, porous, often fluid, and uncertain.

Second, poietic language in telling silence. Poietic language and thought in this book, hopefully, will incline people to let go of *what* the language is talking about and will incline them to let what the language is talking about reveal itself on its own, as it were. The hope is for people to release from objectification what is being talked about and to become aware *in* letting what they are talking about happen as *it* happens.

In both types of poietic activity, experiences of uncanniness, awe, anxiety, fear, uncertainty, and shock have importance equal with conceptual and imaginative formations. At its best, poietic language, thought, and activity are creative, practiced in releasing what is being talked about from objectification, and if fortune smiles, occasionally beautiful.

A final prefatory note on poietic language and activity. The poietic agents—the ones who speak and act—can themselves become poietic events who experience immediately their own transformations; they can live intransitively with awareness *in* a birthing process—perform the process, we might say—as they engage a threshold-occasion of bringing something new into the world or as they are aware of silences and silence silencing without objectification. The process itself then constitutes a poietic moment of transformation for agents who let go of their agency and the objects of their agency. Then people may feel silence *in* silence silencing—feel silence as silence "does" "its" own no-thing.

I will frequently use the term *silence silencing* to speak of silence in "its" unformed presence. Just silence. No identity. Not a thing. Silence happens silencing, we might say. Indeed, the book's guiding issue is attunement with silence silencing, although I will often speak of particular silences that are defined by the circumstances in which they occur, such circumstances as the silence in a cave or in the kitchen. The guiding purpose of the book is to create moments that heighten and intensify the reader's attunement with silence silencing. In such attunements, I believe that people might be inclined to question desires for unchanging and solid foundations that support established beliefs and values. Attunements to silence silencing and predispositions engendered by those attunements

---

5. Usually, affect is used as a verb and effect is used as a noun. I will also use the word *affect* in relation to feelings (affects).

might also diminish the power of those desires. They might incline people to affirm the silent volatility of the world around them, volatility that infuses their being and makes possible creativity as well as experiences of awe in the flow of lives, in the shifting, passing, often unpredictable lives of all creatures.

Inclinations toward unification are so powerful in most theoretical lineages and, I believe, so obscuring of the lives around us! Those inclinations tend to obscure silence silencing. Alertness to silence silencing can interrupt everything including the usually unchallenged value of unification. The universe, for example, when defined as all living things everywhere gives remarkable priority to "things." Silence silencing does not unify or form wholes. "It" does not support images of "the" world or a universe as a whole thing of unified events. "It" harbors no secrets. Silence silencing harbors nothing. "It" is not an it. I will say a good bit about that throughout the book in language and thought that fall silent in awareness with silence silencing.

I engage many writers, poets, and artists in the course of the book, but not always because of what they say about silence. I engage many of these people, rather, because of the ways silence happens in what they say, paint, or build, how they form their expressions, and in the ways their works convey awareness of silence in silence (a phrasing about which I will have much more to say). There are many agendas in works about silence. Although I find some of the works of other authors helpful, many of the writings about silence do not seem to be attuned to silence silencing and have agendas quite different from mine. Silence, rather, is presented as an interesting subject, the absence of sound, an important thing to keep in mind, a fascinating object among other kinds of objects, a path to communion with Divinity.

Or silence is presented as something to cultivate, to bring peace of mind, release from the day's distractions. I find at times, however, feelings of disorientation and discord much more helpful for awareness of silence silencing than peace of mind, a sense of clear orientation, or a sense that silence is something I can come to understand. I can feel estranged from silence by virtue of an orientation that is both normal and at home in my environment or feel estranged from myself and the world around me because of awareness in silence silencing. Silence silencing is not always a friend to normalcy or feeling settled and at home.

When the idea of writing a book on silence began to germinate, I was not entirely sure why I felt drawn to it. I could guess that my desire arises out of my aging and increased awareness of death. But that would not be quite right. I came close to dying several times in my younger years due to illnesses and accidents. I worked in a medical school project on health-care delivery to terminally ill patients and their families in the early 1970s, participated in hospital rounds with doctors who attended severely, often terminally ill patients, and took part in the founding of Alive Hospice in Nashville, Tennessee. For several years I taught an undergraduate course called Death and Human Meaning, in which terminally ill people volunteered to come to classes during the semester and talk with us about the ways they were living with—engaging—their imminent death. I experienced my own mortality up close and personal many times, and awareness of dying as a part of my living is infused in my everyday sensibility. These experiences are alive in the ways they have influenced—deeply influenced—my thinking, and they have a significant role in shaping many of my attitudes and values. They play a usually quiet role in most of what I write and teach; and they will play an important role, sometimes quietly and sometimes, if not noisily, certainly intensely, in this book. But those experiences do not compose my primary motivation for writing about silence. When I become alert to silence, I do not usually feel inclined to think of death.

After cowriting with Nancy Tuana the book *Beyond Philosophy: Nietzsche, Foucault, Anzaldúa*, I considered for several months what I really wanted to write next. The importance of silence—the *question* of silence—appeared far more frequently in my books and articles than I had realized. Why the frequency? Why the silent draw now? Why was I so enticed by the question of silence? Further, the more I thought about silence and the roles it has in those books and articles, the more I also realized that I was not at all sure *how* I would write and think about silence now. How might I write and think about silence without turning silence into an object and thereby turning "it" into an image and losing attunement with silence? How might I write of silence in such a way as to let it be its own telling? Would I *interpret* silence? Could I write of silence non-interpretively? To explore the question of how silence might relate to interpretation, I wrote "Interpreting Silence?" for The North American Society for Philosophical Hermeneutics.[6] Fragments Nine, Ten, Eleven, and Twelve are influenced by that article.

I became convinced that only "interpretation" by indirection is appropriate when the issue is silence. To *explain* silence would be in effect

---

6. Presented in October 2019 at the University of Oregon.

to flatten "it" out so that silence loses its strange elusiveness and seems conceptually clear, one kind of defined thing among other defined things. (The PIE root for the word "explain" is *pele*, to flatten, to make flat.) To flatten silence? To make silence plain and grasp it? To make silence a "clear," well-conceived object so that we can *see* it? *See* silence? What became clear to me was that explanation and visually oriented approaches would not help us become more aware of silence. Further, *making* intelligible would be a misleading intention regarding silence. To make silence anything would be silently to miss silence. Perhaps hermeneutics, when it is understood as an *art* of interpreting, has some promise in speaking about . . . not speaking about silence but speaking about approaches to silence.[7] I will take up this issue in Fragment Nine.

As I considered how to write this book, I read a variety of discussions about silence. I appreciated the quality of most of the scholarship and thought as the authors I read gave accounts of silence in other cultures, in religions, in peoples' theoretical works, or as they wrote about why silence is important in our lives. I wanted, however, to write differently from what I read and to think differently from the way I had been thinking as I spoke of silence. "Something" was missing, "something" hovering beyond what I could conceive, "something" I could not quite reach. I could feel the lure of it. But I could not think it.

"Beyond what I could conceive." To *conceive*, as I use the word, is to form a notion in a person's mind, to *form* an idea, or to *take* something into one's mind. To *convert* silence into a mental form? To *take* silence into my mind and *make* it into an ideal object, *a thing* of the mind? The limits of conceiving silence became the threshold for me to a different awareness, different from anything I had previously sensed. To conceive silence began to feel to me a violent, wrenching action. *What* is silence? Not a thing, not a what. What does silence silencing do? Nothing. I had not previously turned to the question "*How* does silence happen?" Not the question "What are the circumstances that define this particular silence?" But rather the question of silence beyond the borders that bind a silence in a place or situation. I needed an approach that is attuned with silence in silence's happening, one that lets silence silencing tell of itself beyond conception, hearing, or seeing. The intransitive middle voice sense of the phrase, silence silencing, means that "silencing" does not have the active

---

7. The root word in *hermeneutics* is Hermes. The utterly disordered myths of Hermes and those of Metis will function in Fragment Nine as strange and unexpected guides on our way to the immediate sense of anomalous silence.

verbal sense of silencing something or someone by, for example, turning off the volume of sound or silencing a person who is talking too much. Nor is silencing the object of a transitive verb or a subject that receives an action (in a passive voice formulation). Instead, I could say clumsily, silence happens as silence . . . silence silencing. In the context of this book, speaking of the happening of silence is, *as it were*, a subjunctive contrary to fact. "It" "is" not a fact. When I speak of silence's happening—of silencing—I speak in an irrealis mood. I say "as it were" as an irrealis adjective, a subjunctive mood that destabilizes the sense of temporal existence that the word *happening* conveys.[8] Silence silencing is not a temporal happening. Elaboration of that statement will happen frequently in this book.

I want to develop language and conceptuality and to tell stories that are attuned with silence silencing and guided primarily by that affective attunement with silence silencing. What I want to say requires that I speak of silence without making silence the object of such an action as *attune*. So my intention is to be attuned with silence *in* silence, not, as it were, standing outside of silence and speaking sensitively about it.

I have said that silence silencing does not happen as a specific thing. To clarify that statement, I emphasize particularly the importance of recognizing *situated silences*, located silence like silence in the cellar, silence in the dark stillness of night, the silence of the one who will not speak. In situations like these, the circumstances mark the situated limits of a silence, give it a name particular to boundaries that mark it. Silence in the cellar, for example, is called *a* silence because the phrase, silence in the cellar, situates silence. Silence in the cellar, not in the garden.

When I speak of silence silencing, on the other hand, I am referring to silence as silence without boundaries that mark it and define it. I am not referring to a situated event that is characterized by silence. I will say more about the immanence of silence silencing in specific silences in Fragment Fifteen ("Touching Silence") and Fragment Thirteen (last subsection "Silence, Silence Silencing"), where I use the term *sticky silence*.

I occasionally use "anomalous" when speaking of silence silencing, a word that connotes *deviation from what is normal, atypical*. I might say silence silencing is anomalous as it does its own thing. The aggravating problem is that silence silencing doing its own thing isn't *doing* anything or being anything. Silence ("happens") as ("its") own ("occurrence") as

---

8. *Irrealis*, when it is applied to a verb indicates that an act or state of being is not a fact. In English, *irrealis* can be expressed through the subjunctive mood as a statement contrary to fact.

neither a subject nor an object—silencing, beyond the bounds of discursive rules and literal good sense. One of the guiding thoughts in the following fragments is that silence silencing is anomalous in its lack of identity. Silence silencing [is] not something. Silence silencing [is] no thing, and silence silencing pervades our lives, the lives around us, and all the spaces in between.

 Chaos and order happening together constitute one of the recurring issues in this book. *Order* derives from eleventh century Latin, *ordo* and twelfth century French, *ordre*. Those words variously mean series, arrangement, pattern, routine. They carry the connotations of uniform, established ranks and proportions, and proper sequence. *Chaos*, on the other hand, derives from the Greek word, χάος that is translated as formless, void, emptiness. It suggests "to be wide open" and "absence of order." The other connotations of the word are lack, absence, hollow. It, the word *chaos*, is appropriate for silence silencing. Although silence might happen with all manner of things and formations, such as a conversation that falls silent or a well-timed silence for effect, or a silent street, or in an empty room, silence silencing [is] formless, void. For now, I want to emphasize that silence [is] no thing, [is] without order, and yet [happens] with formations, with identifiable things: chaos and orders happen together. Chaos with orders, and orders with chaos.

Tantalizing Silence Silencing: Riffing With "Of Mere Being"[9]

Tantalizing is a word that suggests baffling and alluring, drawing and vexing. The word also describes a frequent feeling I have in awareness in silence silencing and the ways such awareness often stimulates and provokes imagining, provokes, for example, the image of a tree, a bronze palm with a beautiful phoenix singing a strange song. "A gold-feathered bird / Sings in the palm, without human meaning / Without human feeling. . . ." A palm at the very edge of imagining, beyond all thought as though verging—teetering—at the end of space. The palm and the phoenix blend oddly in silence without meaning or feeling. The palm on the verge of nothing, "The palm at the end of the mind." The tree fades as a breeze seems to linger in the branches, seems almost to pause before passing to nothing. I seem to be withdrawing from the tree and the bird in the image from

---

9. "Of Mere Being" is one of Wallace Stevens's later poems, collected in *The Palm at the End of the Mind* (1979), 398.

the image. I want the image to brighten. I want to indwell the image at the silent ending of my mind, to feel the breeze, to touch the tree.

"Of Mere Being" does not speak directly of silence or of anything unimagined. It—the poem—is one of imaginative indirection. It speaks *at* the end of the poet's mind as it speaks *of* the end of the mind, of a song beyond thinking, without meaning, without human feeling, without order's rule—a song at the edge of its own imagery. It is a poem of joy just where joy ends. Who would not feel the joy? Stevens reaches the end of reason's sway, beyond sense, and just at this limit on the edge of space, where sheer foreignness happens, a sun-bronzed palm rises. In his poem, the gold-feathered bird in the palm sings a strange, foreign song, a gift of imagination at the edge of imagination, singing beautifully on this boundary, perhaps like the beauty of the poem, singing absurdly in the ending of imagination's reach. The poet is taken up into the song in the tree on the edge of space. "The wind moves slowly in the branches." He sighs, smiling. Silence, mere silence beyond the poem   beyond every   thing

In the poem's wake I am tantalized, enticed to go beyond my reach, beyond feelings as I seem for a moment to be on the verge of dissolving into the poem, not quite hearing the golden bird, but feeling very much at the edge of the orders that form the poem and that form me as I, reading, seem weightless, deforming   at an edge   where the sun-bathed tree   does it stand?   The golden bird   singing?   I cannot quite hear the notes   or see   the tree beyond Stevens's poetic strong soft mel   ting words . . . those words . . . silence in them.   The elusive disappearing of tree and bird   they did appear, didn't they?   I seem to float   to float in the words' dissolution   and yet

I do not know exactly where I am. Am *I*   imagined? I seem to feel a breeze coming from no where   do I sense mere silence as the images fade and I think   I think?   At the edge of the mind?   A bird   singing?

I feel lost. Everything is so quiet. I want the phoenix to return. And the bronzed tree. I want the breeze. *I want to feel that breeze*   I am tantalized   at the end of my mind   before nothing I can say   as words gently melt in silence   in silence   the tree stands   the bird sings

How will I speak of such things to you?

FRAGMENT ONE

Intimations

Telling Silence

> If a writer knows in advance what imagination must be to be imagination, they have already lost an important part of their imagination.[1]

I am using *telling* in the sense of having a revealing affect (a telling smile, for example, or a telling sound in the closet) and also in the sense of putting expressions together in such ways that their affect is to give way to silence's telling . . . to silence's disclosure of, as it were, "itself." The two senses of telling apply simultaneously. I could put the point by saying that silence "tells" of itself thanks to the way expressions are so crafted as to occasion telling moments.

Indirect and *performative dimensions* of communication can refer to such everyday experiences as "the way she blinked indicated to me that she was lying"; or "I could feel his desire for her while he talked to her about cold nights in Kansas." In these examples—*blinking* and the *way* he talked about cold nights in Kansas—each composes a performative dimension of the conversation, an indirect disclosure of something not directly said.

In the following fragments my hope is that direct descriptions, stories, works of art, and statements that I use will constitute telling events and compose situations of indirect communication. I intend for them to communicate in ways that encourage a reader to become aware of silence's

---

1. I have heard Vincent Colapietro say something similar to these words when speaking of imagination. Neither he nor I have found the sentence written.

own disclosure. I hope that this way of communicating, this telling way, also encourages readers to think and feel imaginatively and metaphorically, to be predisposed to words and events that make available what cannot be said directly. In telling silence, expressions do not capture silence in literal sense. Rather, they can open the way to performative happenings in which silence silencing is immediately sensed. *Silence silencing* transmits unspeakable silence silencing. We might say, "our definitive formations are broken in speechless disclosure."

I hope you sense that attunement with silence silencing creates a threshold to ether-like non-place in our lives. Not a dimension of difference "up there somewhere," but mere silence in our lives now as we live our lives. Attunement with silence silencing can affect something like spiritual trembling, a pervasive uncertainty in the heart of certainties, a bit like a dream, an odd—a very odd—dream entering your firm-feeling everyday life and affecting a sense you cannot name. Seeming-to-dream/seeming-not-to-dream together can open people to more "world," more reality than we otherwise have known. Attunement with silence silencing in our lives can affect unexpected changes in our lives, frightful in our awareness *in* all the silence silencing we do not hear as we listen to trucks roaring on turnpikes and birds singing at dawn. Attunement with silence silencing in our lives can also affect a new enlivening, an *ek-stasis*, a standing out in our ordinary living from our ordinary living, a sort of in-spiriting in our opening to new intensities as we come to know that we people are *really* nomads always on the way to discovering who we are to be.

FRAGMENT TWO

The Vastness of the Sensuous

A colleague of mine speaks of people's being drawn into the vastness of the sensuous and releasing "things from worldly logics, including temporal ones."[1] "The expanse of the sensuous, then, enables multitemporal determinations in which there is no overriding sequence, no event[s] that [are] prior to one another, absent the present" (n.d., 10).

"The vastness of the sensuous." A young woman slowly eating a sandwich under a spreading, shading tree at the edge of a field. The tallgrass in the field stretches out to a bluff that roughly frames a horizon. Her "Lover's Bluff." She feels her first kiss with Jim. A summer's day, a breeze. She hears rustling leaves. Buzzing cicadas. Birds chirping, warbling. She sees puffs of billowing white clouds slowly, randomly shape, fade, reshape. Memories mingle with the tastes and smells of her sandwich made of whole wheat bread baked by her grandmother with slices of chicken and tomato. She is dreamy, unfocused as she smells the sweet, lemony fragrance of grass. She adjusts her left hip that rests partially on one of the tree's exposed roots. Her senses happen without direct reflection. In this moment she is living without a sense of measured time or ordered sequence—she feels the sun's warmth in the shade as she sees Jim's face draw closer to hers; savors the tomato-chicken-bread tastes of the sandwich, feels herself a little girl as she smells her grandmother's bath powder, feels the tree's hard root, smells the mix of scents carried by the breeze, hears the cacophony of the

---

1. My colleague, Omar Rivera, said these words at a meeting of The North American Society for Philosophical Hermeneutics in a talk entitled, "Cataclysms: Elemental Exposures of the Cosmic Past." They later appeared in *Andean Aesthetics and Anticolonial Resistance* (Bloomsbury, England: Bloomsbury Publications, 2021), 92.

birds' chorus. She feels the blue sky's endlessness, the clouds' softness, the tree's shade, its standing shelter above, her grandmother's caring presence in the bread . . . Jim's hand on her cheek, the murmur of tallgrass, Jim's moving hand . . . all the sounds, scents, images, feelings . . . memories mingling together . . . a feeling of indifferent timelessness.

It's not that lives and events stand still. She does not sense passage. Only presence. "There is no overriding sequence." Released from logic, explanation, judgment in the intermingling flow of her senses—where she is as she is. All the memories and associations are immediate in her sensations—those immediate memories and associations, their happening in their presence and reach in her awareness, are silent. Sensing, where no words enter, no logic rules, no grammar restricts. Her sensing keeps silence in her sensing. Silence in the midst of sounds. Silence, neither a subject nor an object, without countable time, with meanings but without Meaning. Not a silence between things and senses. Rather, silence in-between. Silence infused in sounds. Sounds infused in silence. No conjunction. Silencesounds. Infused in the woman's senses.

FRAGMENT THREE

Connie's Walk in the Forest

"Connie walked dimly on. From the old wood came an ancient melancholy, somehow soothing to her, better than the harsh insentience of the outer world. She liked the *inwardness* of the remnant of forest, the unspeaking reticence of the old trees. They seemed a very power of silence, and yet a vital presence. They, too, were waiting for the end; to be cut down, cleared away, the end of the forest, for them the end of all things. But perhaps their strong and aristocratic silence, the silence of strong trees, meant something else" (Lawrence 1928, 74–75).

Or perhaps it meant nothing at all.

"She followed the track . . . in the silence of the windy wood, for trees make a silence even in their noise of wind" (Lawrence 1928, 100).

Connie finds distance from her melancholy in the hollows of insentience and lifeless spirit in a dying culture that has lost its soul to industrialization and institutional conformity, to an unceasing drive for wealth and accumulation of goods. She finds solace in the melancholy of "old wood," solace with the trees left standing temporarily in an endangered forest. In the stately remnant she finds silent dignity that shows a strength of standing, rooting, leafing, breathing in the shadow of axes. Rather than insentience, she finds animation—liveliness—a kinship with whatever lives out of itself, lives with what she names with emphasis *inwardness*. The trees and the forest they compose own their inwardness in their "unspeaking reticence." "They seem a very power of silence." In that power they originate "a vital presence." The trees feel to her akin to human passion that in spite of inescapable death craves life, intensity, life-preserving inwardness.

A very power of silence? For Connie, silence's power seems intimate with inwardness. The trees' inwardness in the keep of silence. A power of . . . not of restraint but of sustaining reserve. She might also say "silence in the keep of inwardness." "For trees make a silence even in the noise of wind."

The power that Connie finds in the remnant-forest is one of "an ancient melancholy"—an ancient sorrow of loss—but sentient, inner power, nonetheless. With the trees she feels the *happening* of life-giving energy, a sadness that is *vital*. So different from the soulless culture that surrounds her outside of the forest and leaves her in a spiritual desert. In the forest Connie finds melancholy that struggles to survive as each tree strives—strives with dignity, she says—to be its own and to endure, not festooned with shallow gaiety in the hollows of her social world. Among the trees she finds vital, unspeaking reticence interlaced with silence that gives her to feel alive in her reverie of melancholy.

FRAGMENT FOUR

A Silent Gap's Power

There is always a gap, an opening, in my paintings.

—Alejandro Vallega

Alejandro Vallega recalls vividly the brutal military coup of 1973 when he was a child in Chile.[1] It was a time of horror, shock, terror, and disorientation. The paramilitary was an unofficial force, sanctioned by the Pinochet government and by groups of radical, right-wing people to carry out their brutal ways of ridding Chile of people who were opposed to Pinochet—intellectuals, religious and political leaders, and others who were sympathetic with democratic societies. The paramilitary tactics included arrests, kidnapping and "disappearing" people, barbaric torture, and other forms of inhuman intimidation. Vallega's family, their friends, and acquaintances, suffered the manifold results of these tactics, as the violence and its ever-present potential happening permeated their lives.

Vallega was nine and ten years old during this time and old enough to "understand" and feel the shock and disorientation that pervaded the atmosphere; and he was old enough to absorb the pathos and violence—the terror—that came with the atmosphere. "This understanding," he said, "was not only rational. It was also affective, memorial, embodying."

---

1. Alejandro Vallega is an accomplished artist as well as professor of philosophy at the University of Oregon. His paintings bring together darkness and light with empty space and dynamic movements that seem to incline toward and away from a center that he wishes could be there. The Vallega quotations in this fragment are taken from the first four pages of "Silencio Vivencial/Germinal Silences," an unpublished lecture.

18 | Telling Silence

Furthermore, the stories they began to hear were confirmed in everyday life, in the instances of "the military ransacking of our house," for example, "at night while we stood in the living room surrounded by *collafnikovs* [thugs; brutal people with machine guns] and soldiers with empty eyes, whose ultimate aim was to take my father, if not all of us."

Vallega uses the language of Nelly Richard, one of Latin America's most prominent cultural theorists, when he refers to postcoup Chile as a dismembered landscape, a dismembered society, a dismemberment many Chileans (including Vallega) embedded in their physical memory.[2] The trauma bodies forth from silent invisibility as a fracture, a rupture in one's identity and culture, a gap, a silent opening that does not heal or configure anything.

The gap Vallega speaks of when he says "there is always a gap, an opening in my paintings," happens as a silent absence of connection in the midst of many connections. Not only in the paintings, but also in his life—a "life-gap," an absence *with* present things and lives, an empty opening *in* his life as he lives with many present configurations, with himself and his recognized identity. The embodied trauma of the terrifying social and community dismemberment means for Vallega that he is never completely at home: he is fully at home nowhere. He is, he says, exilic, a word he elaborates with the term between-being. "I find 'my' self," he says, "to be a between-being, a threshold participating in/through/with passing moments not corresponding to logical and conceptual categories of binary thought. Here between-being does not mean dipping into two categories, such as western and non-western, male-female, nor does it refer to a dialectical movement seeking an *Aufhebung* or sublation that will resolve ambiguity in a third identity."

The gap silently remains. Resolves nothing. The dash in *between-being* is the sign of the gap, a silent opening of no thing, a threshold without community, while Vallega lives in communities and in cultures. In the gap, he is indefinable, without distinct being as he lives between and not between. He lives the gap of Chilean horror and dismemberment that

---

2. Nelly Richard is the director of Cultural Studies at Universidad ARCIS and vice-rector of Outreach Communications and Publications. During the Pinochet dictatorship she played a major role in *Escena de Avanzada* art movement that resisted the regime's censorship and oppression of museums, schools, universities, and public media. In his discussion, Vallega is referring to the opening two paragraphs of chapter one of Richard's *The Insubordination of Signs: Political Change, Cultural Transformation, and Poetics of the Crisis* (2004).

was bequeathed him, outside of comprehension and meaning, silently and always disconnected in the connections of his life.

And yet. The gap provides an indeterminate opening, a threshold without configurations that can happen also as a "germinal silence." The memory instilled in the dismembered society and wounded individuals need not be buried in silent and "invisible memorial embodied consciousness." The trauma lives on. It will not speak. It cannot be erased. Vallega will always be an exile. People are able, however, to remember what happened in spite of the trauma. He and others who experienced similar traumas are able to do as Vallega is doing in his paper. They can recuperate the events that Chilean officials try to bury. They can tell the stories, gather the facts, take the testimonies, expose hidden horrors. They can transform their lives as they turn into a community of those who explore new directions for their lives individually and together, nonetheless scarred by the gap, by the dash, by the dismemberment that will not fade. Or as Vallega says, "we carry our dead with us, never leaving the past behind."

In the verge of the traumatic events of the past, moving with the gap in one's body . . . in one's flesh . . . as the scarred ones learn how to speak of it, think it, feel it now, they are empowered to engage the strange power of the trauma's interruptive gap, engage the generative possibilities that might arise in the gap's broken wake. In the gap, the powers of authoritative canons, established bifurcations, and unquestioned values are disrupted. Shaken from their hold, those powers often feel to the traumatized survivors questionable and optional. Other options, previously unimaginable, might appear. A new, if always threatened world might silently emerge. Put strangely, in the birthing of an always threatened new world, traumatized people might feel with their transformations a very strange benefit. They might feel inclinations, for example, as Vallega did, toward specific ways of relating, of recognizing and understanding "those who do not fit, those who do not belong, those excluded . . . those ultimately seen as nothing in terms of traditional senses of identity, being, and knowing. . . . In short, those who seem to have no place in binary logics . . . in their very existing [on borders, they] participate in ways of being unimaginable to traditional philosophy and the academy."

Vallega tells of creative transformations that arise out of a gap of nothing, an opening born of suffering and horror. A dimension of awareness that is without bifurcation or justification. Can you feel "it"? Silence silencing pervading the trauma. The turnings, the exposures, the verges of borders, and the transformations consequent to germinal silences?

FRAGMENT FIVE

Being True to Nothing

Hear what e e cummings says as he speaks of "Beautiful" (1991, 713): "unmeaning of (silently)falling(everywhere)s Now."

The strangeness of the poem, its friable, disjointed words, its unspeakable silence, its silent unmeaning as now falls brokenly, beautifully fractured "e/ver/yw/here." Now's falling everywhere in the beautiful meaninglessness of time. Falls, perhaps, like a shower of shooting stars? Like the silence of falling snow on snow when the world feels still? Falling beautifully. Always now. Without meaning.

The falling is porous, not quite sayable, not quite graspable. Not an identity. Not *a* fall. Falling unmeaning. Silence falling wherever here is now. Silently unmeaning falls.

The silence of falling unmeaning now happens as silence revealing silence, as silence silencing, as telling silence. The poem silently gives way to silence as words and meanings fracture and crumble, as overriding sequences disappear and signs are released from logics until the senselessness of the lines allows another kind of sense to emerge—allows an unordered sense of silence.

```
     silence
            falling   every    where
                                   all wheres    now
       every time    all times    now
         happensatonce
       differential      broken
                                  apartblended
          chaos of silence      unmeaning
       often beautiful       chaos
```

Can we accept it? Can we love it? Can we celebrate it? "Beautiful" is true to nothing. *Silence, unmeaning, now* indicate no thing. Yet those words and the other words, broken and crumbly as they are, make a telling difference: "unmea   ning   of(sil   ently) fal   ling." When readers venture into the poem, when they feel their way into the poem's space, they can feel through its fractures of sense and order the untruth of unmeaning silence. Silence silencing   nothing   now

FRAGMENT SIX

Haunting Silence

A Short Excursus

Haunt as a verb now has the sense of to manifest itself regularly or to be persistently and disturbingly present. In its early history in PIE (Proto-Indo-European), however, it probably had a sense of to bring home, to settle, to dwell, to be home. In the thirteenth century the Old French *hanter* meant to practice (regularly), to be familiar with, to visit regularly. By the fourteenth century *haunte* in both Middle English and Old French meant to attend school. It had a secondary meaning of to have intercourse with. *Hanten*, a noun used also in the fourteenth century, meant a frequently visited place, a habit or custom. The reference to a spirit or ghost returning to the house where it lived might have been active in Proto-Germanic, a reference that, if lost, was revived by Shakespeare in *A Midsummer Night's Dream*. In Act 2, Scene 2, for example, Oberon says, "What night-rule now about this haunted grove . . ." and in Act 3, Scene 1, Quence says, "O monstrous! O strange! We are haunted, masters, fly masters! Help!" In the mid-nineteenth century in African-American vernacular *haunts* applied to a spirit or ghost that haunts a place.

◆ ◆ ◆

Imagine you are driving on a narrow backroad across a prairie in late afternoon. Shortly before sundown the temperature gage turns red. The car sputters, jerks, stops. Steam hisses from the engine.

Your cell phone receives no signals. A dead zone.

As you think about your options you open the car's window. Nothing to hear but wind blowing through prairie grass with a low murmuring swishing sound. Murmuring everywhere. Treeless space in every direction. The road opening out, extending into fading distance. Eerie silence haunts the wind's sound.

The low murmuring grasswind accentuates your sense of silence. As though nothing were there with the grass, wind, road, sky. Nothing with you in the prairie's fading light. You can feel the silence as you hear the sounds, sense silence as though wind and grass dwell with silence. Silence persistently, disturbingly there. As though silence owns no-place that haunts the prairie's dwelling place.

Perhaps silence dwells with you? Remains in your dwelling?

Dwelling . . .

Where I dwell . . . where I remain, regularly return to . . . the specificity, the definiteness of where I dwell can lead me astray. When I feel at home and sheltered in my place of dwelling, I might not sense silence throughout that "unseams" and infuses what seems wholly, seamlessly definite. The chair, the window, the picture, the room . . . all interlaced with silent space. I might feel secure at home, unquestionably secure. I might not sense indeterminate silence. I might not sense that home and no-home happen together, that no-home happens at home, that homelessness haunts home.

Consider where you are now. Do you feel secure in the moment? Are you safely situated? Does what you are sitting on feel reliable? Would you now, please, look up from this page, see what is around you? See what is in place. Each thing. Not necessarily fixed in place. Simply placed. Do you feel space among the things? Can you sense silence with the space?

If your mind is awhirl, would you still yourself for a moment? (This is not a lesson in meditation. Just stilling for a short time to allow a wider range of ordinary awareness.) Do you sense silent space pervasive of the room and pervasive of the sounds in the room? Can you feel silence? Silence with things? Silence with sounds?

Another imaginative jump. Envision a vague, shadowy immaterial figure hoovering in a corner of the room where you are. It is airy, fading out and in. It need not be menacing or baleful. Just an indeterminate presence that defies good sense. If you do not believe in ghosts, all the better. I am not attempting to convince you that ghosts are real. The reality of ghosts is an imagined reality. But if you are willing, feel as though a ghost is in the room, that it haunts the room where you are. In your fantasy, does haunting presence change the feel of the entire room? Add several people to the room, people who are talking and have no sense of the levitating presence. Is the ghost more or less accentuated for you in the chatty atmosphere? Move toward it. Is it diaphanous in its presence? Immaterial like an imagined event? As imagined, isn't the ghost real in its intangibility? Isn't the ghost not a thing? Is silence a thing?

The film *A Ghost Story* allows a nameless person (identified as the Prognosticator) to speak in his attunement with the ghostly silence that haunts not just houses but the universe.[1] I will do a riff on part of the Prognosticator's conversation with a small group of people among many others at a loud, artsy bohemian party that is obviously focused on fun for now. The party takes place in what the Prognosticator calls a haunted house. That would be a house where silence happens with everything.

He asks the anonymous woman he is talking with if money and love were the two polarities in her life. Money, he says, is not going to tell us anything important about our *lives*. Love might. It passes away. And time: "time's a big one." They agree that God doesn't happen to make a difference. So what's to live for? To be remembered; to make in your name—in memory of you—a sustained, unbroken difference in the future? "You do what you can to make sure you're still around after you're gone. Since your children are going to die, and their children are going to die, and on and on, family lineages fade pretty quickly in the changing flows of time. Love is nice, and it too fades. But art. That's another matter. Take Beethoven's *Ninth Symphony*. He's writing it, let's say. He's been writing it for God. But he wakes up one day and realizes that God doesn't exist. So, suddenly all of these notes and chords and harmonies that were intended to, you know, supersede the flesh, you realize, 'Oh, that's just physics.' So Beethoven says, 'Shoot, God doesn't exist, so I guess I'm writing this for other people. It's just nuts and bolts now.'

"Maybe there is an art of living. An art that assembles the nuts and bolts of living in ways that figure out what really matters in this one life with others, figures out how to enjoy the truancy of images—all the products of imagination. Images like music, other works of art, beliefs, principles, values, and meanings that are never fixed and can change if,

---

1. The following remarks are taken from the 2017 film directed by David Lowery, but the discussion of them does not assume that the reader has seen the film. All words marked by quotation marks are from the Prognosticator's monologue as it is given in the film.

say, twenty-two chosen notes are crossed out. They can change at the blink of a whim or a wisp of anxiety or the trauma of defeat or panic over mortality or horror before the possibility of being forgotten forever. And maybe part of that art of living couldn't care less about most of the stuff that has to do with legacies for the long term. A couple or three generations would be enough . . . well, maybe five or six. After that it gets fairly hazy. Some of the art, like Beethoven's, lasts much longer. But what's 'longer'? 'Cause by and by, the planet's gonna die. In a few billion years the sun will become a red giant and it'll, uh, eventually swallow Earth whole. This is a fact." Don't you realize that "the universe is gonna suck itself back into a speck too small for any of us to see? All consciousness will be long gone. What's left is silence. Vast silence with that speck (probably those specks) beginning to blow out again and banging out all kinds of vibrations for machines to hear in a trillion years, beginning and banging in silence. So you can build your dream house . . . but ultimately none of that matters any more than digging your fingers into the ground to bury a fence post. Or . . . or fucking. Which I guess is just about the same thing."

On the other hand . . .

Some of us might be particular about the way we bury fence posts or fuck—some of us might find those two activities significantly different—regardless of what the sun and the universe might do. That might be part of an art the Prognosticator in my riff didn't see. Haunting silence is neither enemy nor friend. Living at peace with the haunt of silence and nurturing what really matters in a life are parts of the art.

FRAGMENT SEVEN

Dwelling with Silence

Virginia is going with her husband Wilko, whose dementia is increasing, to a step-down facility where he will stay for the remaining months of his life. Owing to her very alive Dutch heritage, Virginia was particularly careful with everything in her house. All details mattered. With her care for her things, however, came an ability to let go, to release . . . to "dispossess" the following poem says. She loved Wilko. This poem speaks in the resonance of her house, her love, the releasing freedom that arises from her love, and silence in her house and in her life.

Virginia's House

I felt silence in your house,
stillness
almost whispered.
I felt silent space
in-between your furniture,
nothing
in the midst of everything,
in-between the Dutch blue,
Dutch white
china cups and plates
standing behind closed glass
cupboard doors.
I did not know what it meant
until I saw you decide to go with your husband

and dispossess yourself
of nearly everything,
not just cups and plates
but furniture—tables, chairs,
lamps, books, spoons long collected,
pretty little salt and pepper shakers—
memorial things, useful things, precious things,
because they were things
and you wanted to be by Wilko's side.
You could not take them with you.
I felt the silence in your eyes,
determined,
more accustomed to the
pain of loss than I had known,
long memories reaching
further back
than I could know,
sadness stilled by hope,
brightness weeping through
the brown of your eyes,
facing certain death
with time to spare
before its moment.
Time now would not spare
your house
or its things,
things of a lifetime
that no longer can be held.
Let them rattle away
to children's shelves,
basements and drawers.
Let them pass to strangers' hands,
severed from the lives
that made them yours.
Let the house begin again
with other lives.
You too begin again
in love
in a time that does not

spare you in the
stillness
that it gives you
with the silence
that your house
held and knew
for its
time
when it was filled with your life,
the laughter of your friends,
the voices of your children,
the darkness of nights
as you slept
at Wilko's side. (Scott, n.d.)

FRAGMENT EIGHT

"That Silence"

The domesticity of the setting for "Virginia's House" is troubled by mental decline, death's imminence, and silence. Silence is like a crack through which nothing is felt throughout the *domus*, nothing that makes every thing in it disposable. Love, too, troubles her house: love is the force that moves Virginia to give up her house and home. The strength of her determination is firm, almost cold, yet tenderness is one of the poem's defining moods.

An inhuman universe is the "setting" for Robinson Jeffers's poem "The Treasure." No tenderness or domesticity in this rhapsody. No love. Deep beauty, yes, and surpassing joy. But the poem's moods are found in detachment from suffering, values, and mortal anxiety. They are found in astonishment with the vastness of the macrocosm, its matter and space that "are," as it were, infinitely excessive to the world, beyond time, beyond, he says, "what they call life." Beyond activities and their vitality: "Enormous repose after, enormous repose before, the flash of activity." Before and after language. Before and after animation and death. Astonishment with the "before," with the "after." Astonishment with that silence. Silence silencing, the inexhaustible treasure.

The Treasure

Mountains, a moment's earth-waves rising and hollowing;
    the earth too's an ephemerid; the stars—
Short-lived as grass the stars quicken in the nebula and dry
    in their summer, they spiral

Blind up space, scattered black seeds of a future; nothing
    lives long, the whole sky's
Recurrences tick the seconds of the hours of the ages of the
    gulf before birth, and the gulf
After death is dated: to labor eighty years in a notch of
    eternity is nothing too tiresome,
Enormous repose after, enormous repose before, the flash of
    activity.
Surely you never have dreamed the incredible depths were
    prologue and epilogue merely
To the surface play in the sun, the instant of life, what is
    called life? I fancy
That silence is the thing, this noise a found word for it;
    interjection, a jump of the breath at that silence;
Stars burn, grass grows, men breathe: as a man finding treasure
    says "Ah!" but the treasure's the essence;
Before the man spoke it was there, and after he has spoken
    he gathers it, inexhaustible treasure. (2001, 100)

FRAGMENT NINE

Interpreting Silence?

Deviations and Interruptions in Hermeneutics in the Lineages of Zeus's Messenger

Deviations

Interpreting silence turns me away from the priority of language, away from texts and other forms of communication that address silence objectively. Interpreting silence turns me away from the priority of understanding. Among the many meanings that "interpreting" can have, including those like "apprehending" or "comprehending" that have an overtone of seizing or grasping (*prehendere*) will not do. Better meanings for "interpreting" might be "to elucidate," as distinct from "to explain," portray in the sense of "let something become apparent," limn in the sense of "illumine or suffuse with light and make evident." In the jurisdiction of these words, interpreting silence would mean to let silence shine, as it were, in its silencing and not lose a sense of it in the words I use. But these words (*elucidate*, *portray*, and *limn*) that I have used to highlight aspects of interpreting suggest seeing and visibility, and silence does not happen to be seen. Silence is not visible, not a phenomenon that shows itself from itself.[1] We might rather say inelegantly, silence silences silently. Awareness of silence requires awareness with . . . *in* silence's invisible silencing.

---

1. The word *phenomenon* has in its etymology the sense of *phaino*, to show, to bring to light. The Greek, phainesthai, a middle voice formation, means to show itself (from itself), that is, to come to light of itself.

Hence the question mark in this fragment's title. We can certainly speak of silences and of silence silencing; but speaking of silences and silencing in ways that heed silence and do not immerse "it" in sounds, meanings, or formations requires a way of thinking that is different from the ways of thinking that often take place in clarifying, interpretive efforts. Speaking and thinking of silence need anomalous indirection. Indeed, does silence have direction? Does silence *have* anything?

Interruptions

My interest in the question of hermeneutics and the question of interpreting silence puts me in mind of two ancient Greek divinities, Hermes and Metis.[2] Hermes, the personal messenger of his father Zeus was as tricky and devious as he was positively disposed to Gods, humans, and the souls of the dead for whom he was often a guide. Given neither to violence nor to pity, he informed by messages and by making pathways in otherwise indeterminate space. His sign, the often phallus-like herm, marked routes (paths) and boundaries. As Hermes *Nomos* his was the power that turned indefinite land into designated grazing fields for flocks and herds. But in addition to his being the primary messenger of the Gods, a figure of mediation, and the one whose power established borders, he had many deforming powers that showed in multiple guises. He was a God of transgression who would cross or violate whatever was bounded. He was never defined or limited by the borders that he created, and he was never definitively limited by any identity that he assumed. He was the master of thieves, cheaters, and stealth (one might think Hermes had some divine influence in the 2016–2000 White House), and he was a God of rhetoric and special pleading.

He was born to steal, as Apollo discovered on the day of Hermes's birth when he stole fifty of Apollo's cattle. Not even Zeus could trust him. Hermes's boundaries were porous and moveable, and a designated, defined pasture (*nomós*), properly marked by herms, could be protected by laws (*nómoi*) and customs, or it could be ignored and lose its normative definition and distinctness. The pasture could be a space of wandering

---

2. *Hermeneutics* means now the interpretation of written and spoken language. The goal of interpreting is to clarify the meaning of the language in texts and discourses. It can also mean an art of understanding and making oneself understood.

and serve the needs of the "uncivilized," homeless, and randomly roaming groups of people (*nomandikós*) who recognized no binding laws and hence no standardizing boundaries. (The Proto-Indo European root *nem*, the root for "nom," means not only to assign and allot but also to take. This ambiguity pervades the "nom" words in this paragraph.) The meanings of law, boundary, custom, itinerate, nomadic, and unauthorized transgression interfuse with each other—the nomadic people transgress the *nomá*, the boundaries. Hermes figures the power of this restless, unresolved instability and unclarity. His power to establish determinate boundaries and way-markers is also indeterminate: his power can take what it gives or assigns. And *Hermes* is the base word in *hermeneutics*.

Perhaps the serious authority of Aristotle, who authored *Peri Hermeneias (De interpretatione)*, obscured the happy rascality, lawlessness, and airiness included in the lineages of Hermes's power. Within those lineages, to interpret, to guide, to misrepresent, and to mislead have meanings that can interfuse with each other—people can guide by misrepresenting, for example. They are not necessarily at odds with each other.

We interpreters must resist the temptation to imagine the patron God of hermeneutics as one entity who carries out Zeus's orders and who delimits, determines, mediates, and guides. Friendly with magicians and pickpockets, visible only when he (should I say "they"?) wanted to be, a skillful, much practiced deceiver, a fine diplomat when the occasion arose, rather more like a flash of disturbed light than a steady or standing presence, Hermes was not one anything. Further, hethey came to be known (also) as Hermes Trismegistus, the thrice Great God, fused with Thoth (did hethey sometimes have the head of a baboon?) who among many other things transmitted strange messages that only especially gifted prophets and poets could decipher. Lots of amalgamating mergers going on in those ancient days when our lineages were being crafted by random, fusing, often conflicting accidents and myths—Gods with humans, Gods with Gods, Gods with demi-Gods, Gods with non-human animals. Stories and lineages mixed, mingled, and blurred the defining boundaries of identities. These stories and lineages left would-be stable, normalized, but in fact nomadic grammars, meanings, concepts, and rationalities, left them tangled and fractured, left them in the dust of established means of recognition.

I have Hermes in mind due to histheir interruptions of the determinations required for stable and meaningful communication. Histheir lineages fused not only with Egyptian practices but also with multiple senses of "bearer of messages" and "revelation." I believe that Hermes's ambivalent power stirs deeply within the hermeneutic traditions, his laughter echoing in the vast and groundless chasms of silence over which people build bridges of interpretations, interpretations in-formed by the lineages of Zeus's messenger who steals the struts and girders, cables and beams of interpretive structures and leaves their bridging skeleton insecure in the silence that surrounds them.

Another Interruption

On the other hand, stories—and various kinds of fabrication and art—might well indicate indirectly and intensify our awareness of what we cannot say directly. Homer's poetic stories, for example, combined with his lightness of heart, have a performative and intensifying quality. As he tells of events, adventures, and mythical beings in his poetic narratives he figures delight in the telling even when he spins the tale of a particularly violent event, such as of drowning men or the destruction of a city or the rape of a princess. Pathos, empathy, and judgment are usually absent in Homer's poetic telling even as his poetry speaks of pathos, empathy, and judgment among the personae who appear in his stories. A contagious affirmation and delight infuse his story of an event's particularity. His telling brings the event like a flash of light into the darkness of boredom, discouragement, sorrow, or abhorrence of life. It brings the reader to affirmation of life without an infusion of ethical or metaphysical requirements. Homer's stories bring out and affirm a dimension of living that is not circumscribed by the loss, mores, suffering, or defeat that those narrated, sometimes lost souls undergo. I will connect these statements with speaking of silence in a moment.

Consider the story of Hephaestus trapping in a chain netting his trysting, divine wife, Aphrodite, with her lover, the war God, Ares, in what I like to think was an orgasmic embrace. Hephaestus called all the Gods to come and "see what I have here!" I imagine that Hermes's reported laughter and wit were the least restrained of all the reactions in that divine crowd. Hermes, the pitiless, the shameless, the non-reverent one. The amoral. The inconstant. The high-spirited, carefree, and light-hearted one. Appropriate to Homeric telling. Maybe not so fitted for Platonic or Aristotelian sensibilities. Perhaps not entirely suited to Europeanization or Americanization. Not fitted for interpreting scripture or for the guidance of church fathers or rabbis. Hermes, the shameless one whom Zeus appointed to teach people the value of justice and community. Hermes, outside the range of Friedrich Schleiermacher's, Wilhelm Dilthey's, Martin Heidegger's, and Georg Gadamer's thought. Hermes, the multiple one. Hethey, the God so full of deviance, truancy, and devilry. So full of movement, light, and life. So on the go with the complexities, fusions, contradictions, and random interplays in being alive. Hermes, the life-revealing one.

The recent lineages composing modern hermeneutics appear to have silenced Hermes's ancient inspiration. Or perhaps Hermes in those lineages stole his influence from *those* lineages and thus from us hermeneuts. He has, after all, been known to abscond with the conversations of an entire room of talking people and to leave a strange gap of silence behind him. He was known to be the Great, the Great, the Great God. Surely, he could have taken himself out of hermeneutic thought and practice, stolen his own presence. One might say that he stole himself away and left his sillage to drift in the silence he leaves behind.

I am leaving behind the esoteric, hermetic traditions that follow Hermes Trismegistus, just as I am turning out of the paths of theologically inspired biblical exegesis and their impact on recent hermeneutics. I am bringing together Hermes the Trickster with Homeric lightness of heart as I think of interpreting silence. The words *elusive* and *evasive* come to mind. I think of the cultivation of something like a border art that creates with indirection and without an eternal partner, creates figurations of sounds and signs *on* silent borders and not on either side of them.[3] Language with its marvelous and fluid creativity . . . surpassed. Silence. How might I speak of *that*, of silence that is not a that?

No one, I believe, would be tempted to think of Metis, Titan daughter of watery Tiethys and Oceanus, as a wellspring of precise and stable truths, although she preceded her daughter, Athena, as the Goddess of wisdom. Metis's wisdom is fluid. What would fluid wisdom be? Not, I think, a comprehending grasp appropriately called *understanding*. Rather, awareness of and in shifting ambiguities, attunements with fluid and unpredictable transformations, awareness *in* the instabilities of understanding. Her knowledge is not focused by truths, meanings, thingliness, or reliability. Her kind of wisdom happens in the slipping of our grasps as the world's protean, ungraspable, and silent dimensions become evident

---

3. For an elaboration of philosophy as border art, see Tuana and Scott, 2020.

in the slippage. Slippery wisdom? Uncontrolled wisdom in Zeus's belly? Tricky, evasive wisdom?

Finding a language appropriate in its indirectness to Metis's wisdom is not unlike finding a language appropriate to silence. Part of the search requires a shift from the traditional bonding of truth and goodness with clear stability and moral decency. The search requires a shift to the value of uncertainty and indirection. Although I do not expect awareness of and in silence to lead to Metis's wily craftiness, I believe it can lead to shifts in people's basic sensibilities and away from an overriding emphasis on intelligence that is based on formations of reason, understanding, and proper interpretation.

FRAGMENT TEN

Interpreting in Discontinuities

I want to speak of silence. I want to speak of it in such ways that silence . . . not this or that silence, but silence silencing . . . becomes . . . I cannot say becomes audible . . . becomes. . . . No. Not becomes . . . I mean, awareness *in* silence silencing . . . our awareness *in* silence silencing . . . that we feel *in* silence silencing *in* our awareness of silence silencing . . . that we feel . . . aware . . . or . . . I hope that we are aware *in* silence silencing. Aware in silence silencing, silence silencing *in* our awareness. There! That's what I want when I speak *of* silence silencing. I would like for us, you and me, to be aware, really aware, *in* the silence of silence . . . aware *in* silence silencing *in* our awareness.

The silence silencing in our awareness? Sitting alone outside in late night, for example, I hear a car motor in the distance . . . a dog barking . . . a breeze in the branches of trees . . . a door shutting. And *with* these perceptions I am aware of silence. Not the sound of silence. . . . Simply silencing of silence. The sky is clear. I look up. Vast darkness with bright stars. I know that stellar seismology can record the vibrations of stars because different stars send out different waves that astronomers record as sounds. But in the midst of such vibrations, silence. I hear *nothing* with the stars and cloudless sky. No thing. Silence silencing . . . in the night . . . with night-sounds. Silence silencing does nothing   Silence Silence silencing.[1]

---

1. For emphasis I am repeating the following note about the middle voice. I am using the word silencing with a middle voice sense. That use means that "silencing" does not have the active verbal sense of silencing something or someone by, for example,

For us humans silence happens as it were along with sounds but not in continuity with sounds. There is no bridge on which sounds become silence. You have probably heard a distant sound, such as an airplane engine, and listened until it isn't in your hearing, listened into that minute moment when . . . sound . . . silence. A bit like a person's last breath. Living . . . dead. Not blending or fusing, but disruption, disconnection. Silence is not like anything. Silence just happens . . . silently.

Speaking of silence silencing with the silence of indirection is hard. It's easier to find an image, no matter how pre-reflective and vague the image is, and then to speak about it. For example, the image of silence as something encompassing us. "Silence happens all around us all of the time." When I say that, the words are sign-noises, a formed breath, words about silence that quash silence. If I write those words—"silence happens all around us all of the time"—the syntax makes sense. Grant me for the moment that the words are reasonably accurate about silence. Those accurate words might constitute an understanding of silence but not awareness of silence in silence. Silence remains apart. Only . . . silence silencing.

Feelings Come First

Vis-à-vis silence, I believe that in our feelings we feel . . . we *know* in feeling; with silence feeling is first. Not conceptualization or truth or a state of mind without feeling. You might wonder, what does "know" mean—"we know in feeling with silence." "Know" in the sense of live in awareness of silence in silence. Dictionaries have a good bit to say about feeling and feelings. Feeling, for example, can be a capacity to experience the sense of touch, or it can be an emotional perception or reaction. There are many types of feeling and kinds of perceptive knowledge. The feeling-knowledge I have in mind happens as an undifferentiated background in—belonging to—a person's awareness, an awareness *in* difference from any identifiable sensation, perception, or thought. The undifferentiated background *of* a person's awareness—rather more like a pervasive mood or ubiquitous

---

turning off the volume of sound or silencing a person who is talking too much. Nor is silence the object of a transitive verb and in a passive voice. In the context of this book, "silencing" names as it were the happening of silence. I say "as it were" in an *irrealis* mood to destabilize the sense of temporal existence that the word, happening conveys. Silencing intransitively   owns silencing.

attunement. I am speaking of feeling as undifferentiated background *in* a person's awareness, feeling that *belongs to* awareness, happens as awareness in silence silencing. Such awareness is not dependent on the mediation of anything. It is immediate. Vis-à-vis silence, feeling comes first.

Feelings sense silence, but not intellectually or by sensations. Silence . . . no thing. It does not *make* sense, although we can make sense of many contextualized occurrences of silence, such as the silence of looking into your lover's eyes looking at you. Feelings can sense no thing in the midst of things. It's not that silence creeps in, intrudes, takes possession. Silence . . . already here. There is no transitivity to it. No passages, partitions, transitions, or progressions. Just silence. Silence happens as it were of itself, we might say awkwardly.

So silence, just silence, doesn't make sense? And people can sense—can feel—senseless silence? Can be attuned with it? Can be in silence and in accord with it? People can feel—can be non-reflectively aware of/in . . . indeterminate silence? Yes.

Silence silencing. Not oppressing. Not shutting-up. Not making quiet. Just not being. Not being everything or anything. Not being death, not being life. Not being. We can go only so far with words, can't we! But we can feel silence in silence. Feeling comes first. Consider a poem by e e cummings:[2]

silently if,out of not knowable /night's utmost nothing,wanders
a little guess. (1991, 810)

I want to pause with these words: "silently, if," "out of not knowable," "night's utmost nothing," "wanders," "guess." Nothing quite tangible, but felt nothing nonetheless. No clear path. No light. No enlightenment. Certainly not a conundrum. No secret knowledge. Simply, silently utmost nothing without authorial certainty to present it. A little guess silently wanders out of night's utmost nothing.

Yet, in the wandering guess-of-the-uncertain-world his lover's "smile sings." Not a guess. A smile. His lover's smile. Can you imagine the smile, the silently felt, simply, only loving feeling, her smile? The mystery of her smile, smiling silently in the silent if-world, the only guessable, not knowable this world always fading into utmost darkness. Mystery aborning in her smile in the guess-world in the silence in not knowable night's darkness?

---

2. All quotes in the following paragraphs come from a late, untitled poem (1991, 810).

His life smiles in the light of her smile. Dream-voices born in the mystery of the lover's smile, "spiraling as luminous," spiraling upward . . . luminous . . . climbing *in* oblivion. Luminously climbing *out of* oblivion. Climbing in and out of oblivion, both. Voices climbing luminous not so much into heaven. The earth suffices. Less into heaven and more into his death, his "deeper death that becomes your kiss." Deeper death as in the mystery of the smile. The smile becomes a kiss. Singingspiraling voices climbing oblivion, dreams, flowing earth, heavenly flowing earth. Swirling. Dazzling. Departing himself, his coming to pass in her kiss. His deeper death, the gift of mystery, her smile, her kiss, "losing through you what seemed myself," he says. He now finds himself unimaginably beyond what he could have imagined, much less hoped for, "beyond sorrow's own joys and hoping's very fears." Transformation. No words. Feel the silences beyond the words. Silent loss beyond imagining. Silent creation beyond sorrows' own joys or hoping's fears, beyond thought, beyond understanding. Now kissed—so unspeakably taken, taken up, taken down—he finds "the light by which my spirit's born . . . the darkness of my soul's return."

*Her. Her*smiling. *Her*kissing. She is his lovebeyondwords. Beyond sounds. He knows her in *her* light. She is his light in the darkness of the guess-world. She is of the silent mystery that entrusts him to sing.

Is it absurd to consider this poem in attunement with silence? Silence in the preeminence of feeling? So much life in silence. So much feeling in silence.

FRAGMENT ELEVEN

Silence, Really?

I am so accustomed to thinking of real and not real that my brain balks at the prospect of twisting free of that dichotomy. In one way of speaking, "real" means, really is. Real is what's there when you stop believing it. "Not real" means, *really* is not. When I think in the force of this duplicitous bifurcation—real/not-real—I have, without any intention of doing so, eliminated the possibility of opening myself to the immediacy of silence. The dichotomy is like a tripping wire. When I stumble over it, I stumble into a sensibility where such phrases as *beyond* real/not-real, *beyond* reason or justification, sound mystical and thus foolish. That's because in this usage when applied to "silence," "beyond" does not happen as a what or as an opposite to a what. "Beyond" does not meet the requirements of being either real or not real. Rather in this context, "beyond" happens, as it were, as no thing and the word, *really*, becomes an intensifier. Silence silencing in undifferentiated awareness really happens, as it were, beyond the limits of real/not real.

Death . . . silence. Death doesn't do anything. It's not an *it* that acts or enacts or creeps or withdraws or whispers or is like anything else. Not like black holes or pure light. Not like a dark cloak. Not-it does not come. Not-it does not go. Not-it feels the way silence feels. Absence.

Really Silent

The tiny body of a days-old puppy lay where it likely had crawled when dogs killed its mother and siblings. My eight-year-old daughter could see it like a dark shadow, darker than the crawl space's far, dark corner under the porch. The body was cool and limp, soft when I reached out and touched it. I paused. A moment of stillness before I pulled it toward me and put my ear to its chest and heard nothing. Dead, I thought. I inched back out and told my daughter the body in my hand was not alive. We could find a place to bury it. "NO! I'm going to get a heating pad. Rub her! Rub her!" I massaged the area around her heart while my daughter wrapped her in the heating pad. A few minutes later with a tiny gasp the puppy suddenly sucked in air. I felt her heart shudder. Stop. Shudder again. Then began a fast beat. She had been dead. Now, she is alive, again. Breathing! We looked at each other for a moment in silent astonishment. Puppy-blue eyes open. Warm milk in an eye dropper. Breathing with hardly audible snuffles in quick succession. Yet so still.

Two days later the snuffles ceased. The puppy was really silent. We talked a bit about the experience we had during those last days as we dug a hole and before we put the silent body in the silent earth. Then, feeling the silence all around us, we fell silent as we filled the hole and walked slowly back to the house.

FRAGMENT TWELVE

Sensibilities with Silences

When I speak of sensibilities, I have in mind pre-reflective dispositions that incline people in multiple ways toward and away from certain values, possibilities, and states of affairs: perhaps toward carefully protected certainties or toward compassionate actions or toward violent punishments; perhaps a disposition that turns us away from particular kinds of people and foods, or away from racial and gender equality, or authoritarian organizations. Sensibilities engender meanings and mores, satisfactions, guilt, and so forth. They—sensibilities—allow people to make sense of things. The phrase *sensibilities with silences* means in the context of this discussion not only sensibilities apropos of silences, in appropriate regard *to* silences in various situations, but also sensibilities that happen with awareness *in* silences. The phrase refers to sensibilities that cultivate alertness to the meanings of silences in particular situations as well as incline people to notice silences in the immediacy of their awareness in silences.

An example. I was camping with friends in a forested area with many sounds around us, sounds of many birds, a distant waterfall, insects chirping and whirring. As we sat talking early one evening a blast from a shotgun reverberated not far away and had immediate and shocking effects. For what or whom was the shot intended? Were we within its range? *Who* shot the gun? After the explosion, in addition to our shock, all creaturely sounds stopped. No bird calls. No insect sounds. The distant waterfalls accentuated the silence. Really silent for several seconds.

When we talked about our experience of the scary event only one other person noticed the post-shot silence. I don't know if she were generally inclined to hear silences; but she was aware of the silence after the gun shot, and as we talked more about silence, she spoke of the silence of the stars. Perhaps she was also attuned to the silence of the ocean just after a large wave crashes on a beach. And perhaps also to the silence of an ocean's vastness.

Beyond such forceful experiences of silences, however . . . silence silencing, unframed silence, silence beyond the borders of silences, silence beyond Gods and mortals. Unmeaning silence. Mere . . . silence. My hope is that in attunement with silence silencing we might experience a loosened grip on things, we might feel release from the tightness of our hold on things. Release accompanied by unclenched determination *to be*. I hope we might live with our griefs and afflictions with a sense of affirmation, live in our fluid, often violent, sometimes loving, always interactive world. I hope we live, when we are able, with lightness of heart, live with many vexing problems and without definitive answers in the always changing spaces of our lives.

In the happening of such sensibility, I think that Metis might seem to smile . . . vaguely, indefinitely. Hermes? He might try to steal our sensibility with silence and leave us with nothing more than the sounds of mis-leading interpretations.

I repeat deviantly. Interpreting silence turns me away from the priority of language and away from texts and other forms of communication that address silence objectively. Interpreting silence turns me away from the priority of understanding. Awareness of silence requires awareness of and *in* silence's invisible silencing (feeling comes first). Speaking and thinking of silence needs anomalous indirection and a silent question mark after each interpretation.

FRAGMENT THIRTEEN

Discovery in Darkness and Light

Darkness plays an important part in the indirect telling depictions of this book—the darkness of night skies, the darkness of death, the darkness of cummings's spirit, darkness in utmost nothing (where little guesses wander), darkness as a friend to sleep, and, I surmise, occasionally as a nurturer of creativity.

The vignette I am about to present speaks of silent darkness as a site of coming to see and of silent light that blinds.

One evening I sat on a bench in a small, dimly lit park. Children were playing tag close to a flagpole where spotlights were set into the ground and shining upward toward a flag. A little boy, probably four years old, too young for tag and ignored by the other kids, jumped on one of the light's strong glass coverings. He looked down directly into the light, then turned his head toward the darkness outside the park, and after a few moments, looked back down into the light. He did this repeatedly with growing excitement. I realized that the light blinded his vision and the gaze into the dark restored it. What a strange experience! Blinded by light? Sight restored in darkness?

The process went on for several minutes before he ran over to his dad and brought him to the flagpole to see and not see the way the boy could see and not see. Soon the older children noticed the father's and son's odd absorption as they stood on the spotlight, looked down into the light, and then toward the dark outside the park. They stopped playing tag, watched for a minute or two, and began to do the same thing with the two spotlights on the opposite side of the flagpole. In a few minutes a line had formed for turns to discover what it's like to have the peculiar experience of being blinded by light and restored to sight in darkness.

I believe I witnessed something with roots in primeval experience: the complex density of light and darkness and their differential, sometimes inspiring, sometimes frightening or horrifying interplay in symbols and meanings associated with seeing and blindness.[1]

What stirs in the boy as he stands on the spotlight, repeats the process with a child's innocence—as he absorbs the wonderous experience before he runs to his father? What was triggered in his brain as this new, unknown experience holds him in its thrall? Does it give him a unique plateau that opens to interests and questions into which he would grow? A new field of wonder? An unsettlement that for years would subtly disquiet him until, let's say, he finds deep satisfaction when he takes a night course on the science of light? Or does the innocent experience, as he grows older, incline him to mysteries that he interprets in religious terms? Does he become a forester who is drawn to the silence of trees and the filtered light that moves among shadows? A marine biologist who loves deep dives in the ocean? A poet? A man who follows a family tradition, becomes what his father wants him to be, and feels that something vaguely important is missing in his life?

As I thought about this event in the park and mused on some of its possible implications for the boy, I realized that the light issuing from the spotlights was silent although the spotlights themselves made a low buzzing/humming sound (that I could hear when I too stood on the spotlight, looking into the light and then into the darkness). The light was different from what generated the light. The darkness outside the park was also silent, different from the place of darkness. This realization that the light and darkness happened in silence, my growing sense of silence, and now a dawning awareness that the boy's experience might include a silent lineage that affects the depths of his sensibility during his life: all of these factors, combined with my fascination with the boy's fascination, moved me to intensify my memory of the complex event. I wanted to imagine the boy's movements without sound, to "see" him without the sounds that

---

1. I am thinking, for example, of the biblical story when Moses encounters God on Mt. Horeb. God appeared in the fire of a burning bush that was not consumed. In addition to taking off his shoes as commanded by God, Moses dared not look directly at God whose divine light presumably would have blinded or killed him. In Greek mythology both Zeus and Helios, in their brilliance, were dangerous to gaze upon. Darkness is often associated with witchcraft, insanity, and evil, while light is often associated with divinity, goodness, knowledge, and life.

were all around him—the chatter of the children, the traffic outside the park, the voices of people sitting on other benches.

So I imagined in slow motion the soundless images I had in my memory of the child's activity. I now see his eyes squint. . . . Then blink as he deliberately . . . slowly . . . looks . . . down directly into the dazzling light for several seconds. In slow motion he raises his head. . . . Blinks again. . . . Looks away and stares to where darkness is. . . . He looks back, now staring down into the light a few seconds longer than before and again . . . over to darkness.

Discovery. I have witnessed a discovery happening. Happening slowly . . . silently in motion. I sit quietly, amazed. The boy's discovery. My discovery. In the silence of darkness and light.

Light and dark, in their perception and their seeming to blend, are silent. Silent dawn. Silent twilight. Silent day. Silent night. Dawn . . . twilight . . . day . . . night, often filled with sounds in their silence.

Strange to me that even when darkness seems so dark and even if in that dark sounds happen, silence pervades. Darkness infused with no-thing. Blinding brightness too. . . . Silence. . . . Not graspable. Not comprehensible.

FRAGMENT FOURTEEN

Sense of Silence

Sense in one sense of the word means becoming aware of something by feeling or intuition—"I don't know why I'm so cautious around him; something about him is wrong, and I don't trust him." Sense by means of a metaphor, on the other hand, happens with words or phrases that give accessibility to something to which the words or phrases do not literally refer. As people come to awareness of something, whether due to smelling, hearing, tasting, touching, intuition, or metaphor, common sense need not govern; nor do the usual rules of acceptable communication necessarily apply. Sensing in the sense I am speaking of is in the jurisdiction of the sensed, not the jurisdiction of logical, conceptual structures. Things have the odors they have, and metaphors have the senses they have. Metaphors can open to the nonliteral disclosures that emerge by virtue of the metaphors. The sensed stand on their own, we might say.

As we sense via metaphors our awareness is held by the nuance, intimation, and implication of the interactive words. Three examples:

—you are my sun,my moon,and all my stars (e e cummings 1991, 810)

Art washes away from the soul the dust of everyday life. (Pablo Picasso)

Chaos is a friend of mine. (Bob Dylan, 1965)

Metaphors like these require imaginative perception for their communication. When a person understands them, they make possible perceptions beyond the authority of literal verification. Consider, for example, what cummings's line makes evident: "you are my sun,my moon,and all my stars." His metaphors convey silently the intensity of his feeling of love far beyond literal expression, far in excess of friendship, fidelity, or affectionate well-reasoned knowledge. Imagining and feeling *in* the metaphors' silent transmission allow one to sense the poem in the power of his love. That sensing is not interchangeable with other senses. It composes its own particular experience that arises in the poet's literally inexpressible love by means of metaphorical imagining: silent imagining that can generate affective awareness of *this* love, awareness of cummings's fervent love that is literally unsayable and silently communicated by means of the poem's interlaced and formulated metaphors.

In other parts of this book, I have frequently invoked imagined things and situations as a basis for sensing, for poietic sensing in which people in their imagining might sense what is otherwise not sensed, something quite different from unimagined occurrences. In this watery region of sensing, hints and possibilities might emerge, indefinite senses of what might become definite—or sense something really indefinite *in* one's sense of what is really definite. In both cases, one experiences intimations of what might yet be possible, intimations of the possibly actual. Such sensing can create a patina of inconclusiveness, incompleteness, and uncertainty throughout our familiar world.

When we sense silence with the prairie breeze or the haunting presence of silence in a room, when we sense no-place in a place, no dwelling in dwelling, when we sense definiteness infused with indefiniteness, we might well think that random unorder—silent chaos—inheres in the orders of our lives and the world around us. Reality then might seem frightening, tenuous, nebulous—cloudlike and not governed by stable Meaning and Purpose.

Bob Dylan, however, said, "Chaos is a friend of mine."[1]

When people hear the word *chaos* they might think of the world around them, a political situation, their sock drawer, their kitchen, their lives. . . . They might think of messes that need to be cleaned up or

---

1. Although I will refer to a few of Bob Dylan's lyrics, the following comments on his metaphor are mine and not intended as an interpretation of what he thought.

straightened out, black holes in the universe, living without purpose or with unanswerable questions about death, freedom, war, suffering and starvation (lives blowing in the wind; life: on your own like a rolling stone).

Dylan is a creator, a restless creator, who forges new directions and possibilities for his lyrics and music. He experiments continuously without a clear, long-term purpose or plan in mind—a bit nomadic, a bit like a rolling stone looking for music yet unborn, but also like someone who finds an intensified sense of being alive and finds his life silently renewed when he undergoes the nascency of rhythms, words, and sounds combining as never before. I believe his experiences of silent creative discovery energize him—vitalize him—make him hungry for more. The burgeoning process holds the silence in the coming of the yet to come. Dylan bears the creation. It is not totally his. From one perspective, he is silently taken beyond himself in the creation he undergoes. In that ek-stasis, the silence in that ecstasy, that silent standing out beyond himself, he finds . . . not himself-in-stasis but himself-in-transition, losing himself-in-the-birthing and finding himself changed in music, in songs.

I believe that creative experiences and the search for them gave birth to his never-ending tour, to his musical life, to his continuous movement in the silence of music-not-yet. His life is a life of music-coming-to-be that is always enticed by and entering the silence, the chaos and indeterminacy of yet-to-be. The incompleteness of his music bears witness to his friendship with chaos. In his sense of chaos he has a sense of silence and finds meaning for his life in that silence. He finds meaning for his life in his sense of silent not-yet.

"Art washes away from the soul the dust of everyday life."[2]

As I consider a sense of silence that can happen in creative artistic experiences, I turn to the Guggenheim Museum in New York City. It is a place for the display of art that is itself a work of art by Frank Lloyd Wright.[3] When people become attuned to the museum's own space and

---

2. The following discussion composes a riff on aspects intimated in Picasso's statement.
3. Hilla Rebay was the founding force for the museum. Her patron, Solomon R. Guggenheim financed the structure, which was described by Ms. Rebay as a "temple to non-objectivity." See *Art of this Century: The Guggenheim Museum and Collection* (Kren et al. 1997, 121).

movement, I believe they will experience what I did: they will be taken up in an experience that considerably exceeds the limits of their subjectivity, a non-objective experience, an experience of imagination. They find themselves in and as a part of a work of art.

The museum's single cantilevered spiraling ramp encircles a vast atrium and takes a person up and up as though on a Parmenidean Way (I use Picasso's language) in one's soul, a way by which one goes beyond the noise, turmoil, emotions, and concerns of everyday life. It is made to engender a process toward spiritual purity, a process toward abounding silence with neither subjects nor objects, a process toward another dimension in human life.

Moving up Wright's spiral can be a wonderfully dizzying experience as distance from the floor increases without stairs and as vibrations of many sounds resonate with decreasing intensity through the yawning open space. As you move upward, spacing out is easy, and if you are close to the edge of the spiral and look at one thing on the floor below while you move upwards you can feel that thing change, diminish in size and shape, seeming to transform silently in the heightening force of the spiraling flow, as though you yourself were a transfiguring power. Or, if you keep your eyes on the central dome high above as you move, a sense of earthly grounding melts silently away in a state of mind somewhere between ecstasy and sickness. As the movement intensified in my experience of it, in the spiraling, undulant, silent space of non-objectivity, and as sounds faded, I felt something that I could name a shift in my world, a world-shift. Undulant space seemed infused with waves of more and less intense quiet that faded in and out with waves of sounds. As I think about this experience now, I recall deep diving in the Pacific Ocean and seeming to flow in a strange and compelling world with only the sound of my breath and with a sense for neither purpose nor the threat of death nor life as I had known it. My feeling was one of just now, only now. Both ocean depth and Guggenheim height can engender such singular and strange affectivity.

But I also had a strange, distinctly non-creative experience when the dust of everyday life became a thick layer of dirt in that great structure. When I was in the Guggenheim's Reading Room and working on a paper on art, repair on the building was in full throttle. The infrastructure of the walls was deteriorating and replacing it without changing the building's shape and integrity was a long and difficult process. The second day I was there, reading and writing, a team of able workers began what I thought would have been a delicate procedure of reaching and replacing a part of the weakened metal skeleton buried deep within the concrete façade. They all, however, used jackhammers exactly as they would have done had they been on Eighty-Ninth Street and digging for a leaking pipe, except they were high off the ground and on the building's upper wall. The chorus of the vibrating sounds they produced was carried throughout the museum by the resonant, yawning atrium, designed as it is to give sounds, like notes of color, free range in their spiritual ascent to soundlessness. The high-speed banging, the rat-a-tat-tat sounds of the jackhammers coming through the walls high up above the spiral rioted down the space, bouncing off walls and tumbling to the floor where they seemed to bounce back, strangely renewed, to begin an ascent that was hampered only by a cascade of new, ear-splitting jackhammering noise from above that was hell-bent to make it to the floor for, I assume, the sake of having its turn at the empowering bounce back up. The downward falling sounds mixed and mingled irritably with the echoing upward moving sound-crowd where they met a new competitor for auditory jurisdiction.

The museum had installed a "shapes in space" exercise for teenagers in a good-sized room facing the second spiral that was designed, I believe, to give young people a sense for dynamic form and color that is complemented by music and physical movement, to provide, perhaps, a link to an aesthetic side of themselves and to give them an inclination to a more artistic sense of their bodies and the world around them. The floor was made of squares of brightly colored panes of light that flashed off and on in random patterns and the kids attempted to dance to the colors with multiple strobe lights flashing around the room and hip-hop booming from strategically placed speakers. There were no doors on this space to contain the sounds of music. Rather, the stereophonic notes flowed out and into the rotunda where the jackhammer notes were in total anarchy, and together they composed a considerably different experience from that intended by Wright. The hip-hop music entered enthusiastically into competition with the jackhammering but lost by the fourth tier where it was totally assimilated, although not without having added its bit to the remarkable cacophony. Also joining the competition were the sounds of several school bus loads of excited children entering and noisily scattering on the ground floor. They were led by startled teachers who doubtlessly came there to enrich their students' education if not their souls.

When I set aside my writing and walked up the spiral ramp in the jarring discord of sounds, I wanted to undergo Wright's spiritually oriented work of art, an architecture that embodies a sense of silence. I wanted to be transported beyond the uproar. But that art actually enhanced the noise and turbulence that it was designed to go beyond. Its lovely acoustics allowed the cacophony to seem to overwhelm silence, to engulf it, and to seem to turn the art against its own intentions. It is a wonderful space, designed to go well beyond the deposition of the "dust" of everyday life (as Picasso used the metaphor, *dust*), certainly to exceed the soul-dusting of superficiality, living-by-trivia, and the racket we can forget that we are hearing. Designed as the architecture is, it enhanced something like a dust storm of noise rampaging throughout the museum and up to its highest pinnacle. Yet, in that enhancement the art that the building composed endured and turned the noise into a temporary invasion, a transgression. The architecture's integrity, its silent, singular power, held the cacophony. The sounds of repair and the loud beat of hip-hop could be taken without offense and lightheartedly due to the structure's spirited creation, its spiraling movements to silence in the presence of so many works of great art. In its inspired immediacy, the dynamic structure itself as a great work of art embodies awareness of the silent force that experiences of creativity can have, the force of silent yes-experiences that, far from discouraged by the dust of everyday life or the cacophony of jackhammering, comprise moments that feel like ever and, regardless of suffering, give birth to feelings that embrace hope native to senses of silent nativity. The astonishing reality, as I felt it, is that this "temple to non-objectivity," as it held both the cacophony and the works of art, also harbored silence and movement toward silence in its—Wright's architecture's—silence. The opportunity to feel the silence in the midst of jarring noise is part of the non-objectivity, the art, the physical poiesis, that Wright's structure silently offers.

I returned to the reading room smiling. I had accepted the architecture's silent offer and had experienced one of the most moving aesthetic events in my life.

Deserted Bones

Georgia O'Keeffe, speaking of her paintings of animal skeletons on the Black Mesa desert in New Mexico, said, "The bones seem to cut sharply to the center of something that is keenly alive on the desert even tho' it is vast and empty and untouchable—and knows no kindness with all its beauty" (Turner 1999, 123). She has a sense of intangible interweaving in the desert of bleached bones and something indifferent to lives but nonetheless is "keenly alive." Not something she can directly understand, but a sense she can paint, her sense of that silent deserted presence with endless sky, plays of shadows and bright light, profound darkness and brilliant moons, all infused with silence in their happening. The bones appear to mark absent lives as they, the bones, "cut sharply to the center." The bones *are* in keeping with the desert in their grave severity and, for O'Keeffe, in their uncanny generative power. O'Keeffe feels that severe power as though she breathes in its inspiration when she creates a real, uncaring, and beautiful painting that comes to life in the absence of the desert and the bones that it presents. Her desert paintings, created with her intangible sense of them, also cut to the center of something that is silent and keenly alive.

As I wrote those words, I would have liked to feel at least a bit of the keenly alive "something" on the desert that the bones cut into and that O'Keeffe sensed. I believe I experienced a sense complementary to O'Keeffe's when I stayed a few days in the Chihuahuan desert. I did not see bones, but in the night's cold, moonless darkness with the distant sounds of coyotes yelping, barking, and high-pitched howling . . . followed by silence . . . desolate silence I felt . . . silence that was vast, empty, and untouchable—*that* silence seemed to meld with the unearthly, uncaring velarium of stars as though they, in their lightless surround, touched a kinship with the desert, totally beyond formulation, in ghostly, shadowless emptiness that seemed alive, very alive in its merciless and soulless beauty.

But I could only imagine O'Keeffe's experience silently . . . at a distance. I must begin with the absence of that "something" on the deserted, the silent space of the desert, and begin with the absence of the artist as well. Further, I had not seen for many years any of the original desert O'Keeffe paintings. So, I turned to this part of Fragment Eleven in the absence of the desert, the artist, and the original paintings. On the other hand, I could work with reproductions and with her writings, begin with the presence of her compositions that are also removed from their subject matter. But they are not removed from her *sense* of the desert. She wrote and painted with that sense of the desert's "something" that happens beyond literal grasp and beyond direct perception. In her life and her resonance with the desert, O'Keeffe found (sensed) the desert alive in its desertion and made more striking by the silent bleached bones. Those bones "cut to the center," not in the sense of piercing that "something" but in the sense of their reflecting that something on the desert back to itself and intensifying it in its disclosive power, something haunting the deserted bones and those bones haunting it. Deserted bones, deathly and lively on deserted land. Deserted together. That's the way their lives happen, the way they are. O'Keeffe sensed desertlifeboneslife, their lives so utterly silent in their desiccated beauty.[4]

I have suggested a double reflection: The bones in the desert reflect the desert's life back to it, intensify it, provide it with a crack through which the desert's empty and indifferent beauty is more exposed; and the desert reflects the bones' desiccated and deserted presence. Life-in-deathdeath-in-life with bone-deep beauty. Dried out beauty. Beauty in being forgotten. *Being* . . . forgotten. Desertbones, deserted bones. Silent desolate space. At once together, silently alive.

O'Keeffe said that she paints "exactly what I feel" (Turner 1999, 4). Her sense of deserted bones, so excessive to explanation, so nongrammatical—seeming to blanch any meaning given to time—intimates the vast loneliness and silence of the desert, its own utter difference. Even the bones she brought to her desert home remained apart from any domesticity her home might have offered. "I have used these things," she wrote, "to say what is to me the wideness and wonder of the world as I live it" (Turner 1999, VI). "The world as I live it." That would be the world as she moves with it and it with her, as she senses it in its enabling presence, as she feels it—her sense of the world and the things in it, be they bones, flowers, feathers, or a tree at night. I believe that the desert and bones happening together with her sense of them cut sharply to something that was keenly alive in her, that the cutting exposed a kinship between her, the desert, and the deserted bones, something beautiful and far more than she could say, but something that ignited her passion to paint and gave her to open to the world around her, perhaps opening like a desert flower.

When I first saw her desert paintings in various museums and when I lived with O'Keeffe's writings and prints as I wrote the paragraphs you just read, my experience was one with profound silence. Silence seemed

---

4. And in their vulnerability. I gestured to that vulnerability in the first sentence of this paragraph when I said that I would like to have captured at least a bit of the keenly alive "something" in the desert. "Capture" and "kill" are closely connected in this context. If it hasn't been captured by concepts, categories, and projections, it has been captured by "property" and capital. Now, a golf course graces that beautiful area with irrigation systems, nearby hotels, restaurants, winery. A great place to kick back and enjoy yourself. If you're there and lucky, you might even find a half-buried bone.

to saturate my perception as I absorbed her paintings and writings. Her very sensibility brought me to silence, always beyond any grasp of it I might attempt. The hollowness in the deserted space stopped with itself, as it were. Nothing more. Empty, as O'Keeffe said, untouchable, knows no kindness. It gives nothing, not even an echo. And yet that desert with its silent bleached bones, as she presents it, seems so very alive.

FRAGMENT FIFTEEN

Sudden Sparks and Wonders of My Solitude
Silent Creation and Free Spirits

I have spoken of *telling silence* as putting words together in their nuance and insinuations in such a way that they give way to silence's telling of, as it were, "itself." The words yield to silences and to silence silencing. I have also said that telling silence is not primarily a conceptual, visual, or auditory event. One feels silence silencing. Responsive attunement and understanding come later.[1]

We have found that imagining can be an excellent way to open senses outside the authority of daily common sense and deeply ingrained beliefs that turn us away from silence silencing. Imagining can open us to what is left out when literal speech is at its best. Open us to "what" is untamed and lawless and not a what.

Further, we found in Bob Dylan's experience of writing and performing music a continuous, energizing *yes* in his musical life. The indeterminacy he experienced in possibility, the indefinite incompleteness of his life, the absence of a predefined definitive world-order such . . . "chaos" is his friend, he said. His silent friend, I said. When a particular lyrical order began silently to form in his mind and when silently it first began to emerge—when creating happened—he, in that experience, wanted to be, to continue to be. He wanted to sing and play. I believe that he felt reborn in the birth of a new song or new arrangement. Perhaps he understood Friedrich Nietzsche's metaphor: "one must have chaos in oneself to give

---

1. See Fragment One, Intimations: Telling Silence

birth to a dancing star" (*Thus Spoke Zarathustra*, "Prologue," section 5).[2]

I turn now to Nietzsche's description of free spirits, one kind of nomadic freedom, and experiences of creation.

The "my" and "free spirit" in the title of this subsection refer to Nietzsche. To speak of his experiences of creating and silence, I will first pay attention to his understanding of free spiritedness and truth. The motivating questions as we move toward creation in silence are: How does chaos happen in a free spirit? Is what Nietzsche writes about free spiritedness and truth true?

"A new species of philosophers is coming up: I venture to baptize them with a name that is not free of danger. As I unriddle them, insofar as they allow themselves to be unriddled—for it belongs to their nature to want to remain riddles at some point—these philosophers of the future may have a right—it might also be a wrong—to be called *attempters*. This name itself is in the end a mere attempt and, if you will, a temptation" (section 42).

The borders of free spirits are porous. They are unstable and yet silently define the values and meanings in an individual's situated life. For a free spirit these borders, in their instability, can be affirmed passionately as people simultaneously explore options for other ways of living and the possibility of bringing something new into the world, the possibility of thinking and perceiving differently from the way they ordinarily think and perceive. In their porosity, the borders silently shift as new influences and possibilities flow through them. Free spirits, as Nietzsche finds them, are attuned in the silence of an undetermined future that is not bound by established meanings or by a directing purpose. Indeed, as embodied riddles that escape clear objectification, free spirits live in ways that are attuned to the occurrences of lives that are infused with indefinite silence and have no essential determination. Even the identifier, "attempters," composes an attempt, a temptation to intensify free spiritedness and thus to intensify a sense of indefinite unsettledness as Nietzsche does his best to describe free spiritedness. He affirms free spirited identities when he discloses their silent unidentifiable lives. By his failed attempt to identify definitively free spirits, he expresses his own riddled free spiritedness. His

---

2. Translation modified. Unless otherwise noted, all quotations will come from *Beyond Good and Evil* (1966) tr. Walter Kaufmann. I will note in the text the section from which the passage comes. The focused sections are in Part Two, "The Free Spirit," and the last subsection, number 296 of Part 9, "What is Noble."

attempt is rife with inadequacy as a disclosure of who the new species of philosophers are.

So when Nietzsche "unriddles" free spirits with the word *attempters*, he leaves the riddles free of stable identification. "And free spirits *want* to remain riddles," writes Nietzsche. When he introduces the new species of philosophers (including himself) he doesn't identify them clearly. He performs what he is talking about. He does not disturb the solitude that they and he want and that holds the meaningless silence that is honored by their desire to remain undetermined riddles, to remain riddled in silence. Riddlers have chaos in their (I will use a word Nietzsche often uses) souls. Not disorder in their souls. Rather, unorder with silence.

Before we come to Nietzsche's dancing star, consider what he says about truth in section 24. He is playful and in a good mood as he writes these two paragraphs (in contrast to his mood in the upcoming section 296).

"*O sancta simplicitas*! In what strange simplification and falsification man lives! One can never cease marveling once one has acquired eyes for this marvel! How we have made everything around us clear and free and easy and simple! how we have been able to give our senses a passport to everything superficial, our thoughts a divine desire for wanton leaps and wrong inferences! how from the beginning we have contrived to retain our ignorance in order to enjoy an almost inconceivable freedom, lack of scruple and caution, heartiness and gaiety of life—in order to enjoy life! And only on this now solid, granite foundation of ignorance could knowledge rise so far—the will to knowledge on the foundation of a far more powerful will: the will to ignorance, to the uncertain, to the untrue! Not as its opposite, but—as its refinement!"

"Even if *language*, here as elsewhere, will not get over its awkwardness, and will continue to talk of opposites where there are only degrees and many subtleties of gradation; even if the inveterate Tartuffery of morals, which now belongs to our unconquerable 'flesh and blood,' infects the words even of those of us who know better—here and there we understand it and laugh at the way in which precisely science at its best seeks most to keep us in this simplified, thoroughly artificial, suitably composed and suitably falsified world—at the way in which, willy-nilly, it loves error, because, being alive, it loves life."[3]

---

3. Translation altered; the word composed is put in place of the word constructed as a translation for *gedichteten*. I note also that the German word in this sentence that is translated as "science" is *Wissenschaft*. The German word does not refer exclusively

If we read these words for their literal meaning, they say that homo sapiens—people—create all manner of simpleminded responses to unclear, subtle, shaded, and complicated real-life situations. People want solutions, not questionable possibilities, and they create powerful images, formulas for rewards, punishments, and wisdom with power-endowed institutions that enforce their "truths." "Forced-truths" we might call them, "truths" that make the world seem manageable and sensible. Out of this insistent will-to-ignorance comes values, beliefs, authoritative knowledge, punishments . . . foolish cultures and societies whose orders are upheld by such creations as gods, universal moral laws, and truth-discovering reason. The point now is that the driving force behind these fictions is blind desire to enjoy being alive with a sense of "almost inconceivable freedom, lack of scruple, and caution. . . ." The foolish and superficial creations are nonetheless creations. Will to knowledge is refined by a base of ignorance, not-knowing, contrivance. The experience of creating a culture's own world and participating in it, adding "this" innovation and "that" reconfirmation of important truths, even when the fabrications are constructed out of spiritual sand, can be revivifying and exhilarating when people feel the power of their "truths." Stated another way: fabrications that are life-denying can be vitalizing. The formless, silent energy of lives can produce life-denying formations.

Language and its grammatical systems, hypocritical pieties, diametrical opposites, hierarchies of truths, lineages of institutional practices that go further back in our souls than we can know—all such mind-making, shaping powers that infuse our spiritual flesh and blood are at play in these two paragraphs. But we can laugh. When we free spirits are mindful of the enjoyment of vitality that can accompany the foolish, simplifying flights from the ways actual lives happen, we can laugh at the irony of pre-reflective and active systems of life-denying sense as they silently function in our languages and sensibilities and pervert what we want to say. We riddlers live paradoxically in a silent distance *with* the simplified, thoroughly artificial, suitably falsified world found in Western civilization that is the given in our souls (so far). We live in the hold of a conundrum, in the quiet of being unsolved puzzles in the sensible society around us, of being riddles who are in transition and do not want to be unriddled.

---

to the natural sciences. It refers to all forms of disciplined knowledge such as literary criticism, sociology, and philosophy. Our expertise and highly trained knowledge, Nietzsche is saying, are based on will to ignorance.

In the silent indefiniteness of our being that Nietzsche names free spirits, we occasionally are able to experience non-literal, never-objectified, and indefinite dimensions of lives where no formations are complete and all formations are dynamic as they come silently to pass. Can we feel, think, write in our riddled attunement with the riddle of being alive? Affirm our transforming existence in it? Laugh at our own serious search for simple truths when we give way to the temptation of surety in the draw of simplification?

Nietzsche's two paragraphs are free of direct, critical rationality and argumentation. The good-humored observations in them are focused on gaiety of life. Nietzsche expresses that gaiety as he speaks of foolish and superficial creations. In his account of these creations, he does not propose bifurcations based on "opposites." He does not see, for example, those who live by falsifications of the world around them as opposed to those for whom divine power is dead and most moralities express spiritual weakness. Instead of bifurcations into opposites, Nietzsche sees degrees of difference and affirms the enjoyment of those who live by simplifications and falsifications, joins in their enjoyment, albeit his is a gaiety that comes with his description of their falsifications and simplifications. His and their affirmation and enjoyment of life are shaded and differ by degrees. A major difference is found in the intense spirit of seriousness that accompanies their love of simplification, on the one hand, and, on the other, the absence of such intensity in a spirit of seriousness in Nietzsche's discourse about "holy simplicity." Rather than upset, earnest, and serious, he is also a bit tickled by his own unavoidable involvement with values and discourses from which he wants to depart. Laughter and irony displace moral seriousness and slavish reverence as well as hold open the incompleteness of their disjointed lives.

Expert knowledge and the hierarchies of enforced truths that support authoritative disciplines and standards of normalizing practices are themselves porous, changeable, mortal, and historically determined through and through. Although those who want simplifications often present them as based on a universal and unchanging foundation, Nietzsche, smiling, points out that their foundation is "the solid, granite foundation of ignorance." So where do we turn to find the truth? To Nietzsche?

In the quoted paragraphs, Nietzsche writes in a riddling way about riddles and in a bemused, joking way about the values, knowledge, and truths that are often taken to heart with great earnestness or at least with the appearance of serious commitment. He makes no claim to truth or moral virtue, although he does confess that he is likely infected by them and their embodied inclinations to want something thoroughly right, something that gives hope beyond death, something good to live by, something true to know. Both the *value* of truth and the *value* of morality, however, are in question for him. We readers are left with a liminal sense of free spiritedness and with the impression that in our world of continuous change we might consider giving more attention to dimensions of lives that are silently beyond good and evil as well as silently beyond truth and falsehood. A willy-nilly love of life and the errors that come with it, and the stimulus for continuous exploration and experimentation seem to be the only quasi-values left standing in the hazy twilight of unsolvable riddles and thresholds opening into silent nowhere in particular.

In section 296, the last paragraph in the book, a very different-sounding, sad and mourning Nietzsche speaks. He has finished the manuscript. He experienced a process of creation and a growth of awareness as he conceived and engaged the words, concepts, nuance, and indirections that compose the book in their silent interweaving; he found himself participant in creative thinking as lively, spirited formations emerged. Have you had experiences like that? When you felt yourself in movements that were both yours and not yours at the same time? Like an intangible and utterly human event of inspiration when the words and thoughts came to you, new words and thoughts in their alignments and fusing nuance—almost as though they were coming through you and holding you? Or perhaps it happened when you found that by adding two new spices to the sauce a new taste emerged? Do you remember the first taste? Do you then remember the subtle, enlivening experience of having discovered something new and in that sense being a part of its creation? Didn't that experience in its intensity surpass the impact of the sensuous pleasure of the taste? Didn't you want that moment to happen again and again?

The issue now is not so much what is created as it is the experience of involvement in a process of creating.

When, however, Nietzsche finished *Beyond Good and Evil* he found that something wonderful was dying: the silent inspired immediacy of giving birth to the book's thoughts and to the artful presentation of them. Here is what he says:

"Alas, what are you after all, my written and painted thoughts! It was not long ago that you were still so colorful, young, and malicious, full of thorns and secret spices—you made me sneeze and laugh—and now? You have already surrendered your novelty, and some of you are ready, I fear, to become truths: they already look so immortal, so pathetically decent, so dull! And has it ever been different? What things do we copy, writing and painting, we mandarins with Chinese brushes, we immortalizers of things that can be written—what are the only things we are able to paint? Alas, always only storms that are passing, exhausted, and feelings that are autumnal and yellow. Alas, always only birds that grew weary of flying and flew astray and now can be caught by hand—by our hand! We immortalize what cannot live and fly much longer—only weary and mellow things! And it is only your afternoon, you, my written and painted thoughts, for which alone I have colors, many colors perhaps, many motley caresses and fifty yellows and browns and greens and reds: but nobody will guess from that how you looked in your morning, you sudden sparks and wonders of my solitude, you my old beloved wicked thoughts!"

"You have already surrendered your novelty, and some of you are ready, I fear, to become truths: they already look so immortal, so pathetically decent, so dull!"

I expect that many readers do not see the thought in *Beyond Good and Evil* as decent, not even as pathetically decent, or approximate to truth. For Nietzsche, however, worse than experiencing angry disagreement and rejection from others is experiencing the loss of the animation and dynamism that accompany the nascent immediacy of thoughts and images in experiences of creativity.

An encounter with *Beyond Good and Evil* will not exceed literal flatness and will become "so dull" if the words, thoughts, and embedded meanings are not engaged and brought to bear in readers' lives. When, consequent to engaging *Beyond Good and Evil*, a person's way of relating with the world around her is deeply affected, she might well experience new vistas, new prospects for living. Some of her beliefs and values might begin to shift—to transmute silently—before she looks "objectively" at what she is undergoing. Her image of herself might begin to change. She might begin silently to feel herself—her sense of her identity—differently in ways she cannot describe as she feels the possibilities generated by her encounter with *Beyond Good and Evil*. Nietzsche's thinking would not be flat then, even if she passionately rejects parts of what she read. An important part of her experience would not be due to her agreeing with what he wrote or taking what he says literally. The book, for example, is conceived without the power of divine images. She, a careful reader, will sense, will feel that absence and not simply note that Nietzsche says that God is dead. She will feel the absence *in the midst of* the book's conception, mood, and orientation. Nietzsche's laughter often takes place in passages that she would take seriously. She might also silently feel his nonjudgmental experience in his creativity more deeply than she can say. So much happens for her beyond the bounds of literal meanings as she digests the book—or we might say, as her reading of the book digests her in her mind/body and provides a new kind of energy, or, depending on her commitments, a new kind of poison.

Serious readers of Nietzsche, however, often understand his compositions as explainable by reference to influences that play significant roles in his intellectual history, influences from Ancient Greek thought and art, from Hegel and Schopenhauer, and so forth. Even new interpretations, regardless their goodness or badness, are like pictures on an ignored wall if they are not embodied and animated—if they are not lived. Lived, perhaps, in feelings of disgust or engaged critique, or in emotions of admiration and positive appropriation. His thought will become lively through the experiences of the reader. Let the accuracy of a summary of Nietzsche's work lie on the pages in their correctness or error as though in a mausoleum of memorabilia. Aren't many histories mostly unanimated compositions? Like a memorial that stands for the life of a long-gone but once-living event? It's not the truth or error of a formulation or a story that is most important. It's their animation in the embodied life of a mind that counts—the way, we might say, the formulation or story is lived out. In his creation's animation Nietzsche found his dancing star in the chaos of silence that is never quite anything. Perhaps readers of Nietzsche will find their chaos, their non-place of silence, and give birth to their dancing stars.

Thresholds, Always Thresholds

Silence silencing, I have said, is no thing and is without order. "Unorder" and "chaos" apply. There is nothing like silence silencing. However, as Nietzsche has described them, free spirits can be attuned to chaos, to silence silencing, to the silent beyond of beyond good and evil. In this attunement, the riddling existence of free spirits, as Nietzsche describes them, holds completions in abeyance in the thresholds of their lives. Uncertainties and questions hold open their spirits, their souls (including uncertainty about uncertainties and questions about questions concerning *spirit* and *soul*). Free spirits, riddled as they are, silently embody lively affirmations of silence silencing. In that affirmation they oblige themselves to silence. It's an odd kind of responsibility—responding silently with silence.

How do readers embody such statements as those in the previous paragraph? Not by intellectual assent, I said, not without a process of making that assent one's own. Not by an abstract argument to prove or disprove the claims or a search for contradictions or an analysis of the history of claims like those in the previous paragraph. The *feelings* underlying and motivating such arguments, searches, or analyses would be sites for animated embodiments. Anger and revulsion would certainly be lively, physical responses. So would the feeling of incredulity without judgment, or experiments to find out how one might be a free spirit as Nietzsche describes free spiritedness, or a search for free spiritedness in ways alternative to Nietzsche.

Another kind of appropriation could happen with a focus on creative experiences. Free spirits, for example, often make their lives explorations into unknown *geistige* (somewhere between "mind" and "spiritual") territory without clear paths to follow or confirmed destinations to seek. Moving into a liminal spiritual space, uncertain and porous as it is, is rather like entering into a never-ending threshold. Those turning into this dimension of life might learn to laugh as they live with definitive values and meanings while the power of some of those definitive values and meanings fades and others mutate with different values and meanings in a kind of spectral mating. Embodied, unordered spiritual procreation. They—these free spirits—feel the sparks and the wonder of new beginnings, births of new prospects, the emergence of thoughtfeelings—bodythoughts that laugh to be. These puzzling free spirits might feel gladness of heart accompanying the anxiety and often the suffering they experience in what seems to be continuous processes of becoming . . . being themselves riddles, creative and often stumbling events infused with the chaos of silence silencing.

FRAGMENT SIXTEEN

Breaches of Divisions

Silence happens in so many ways. In specific contexts, silence is identified by the formations at the site of silence—in *these* situations, in *this* area, in that conversation, by formations by the power of *those* mores and systems of justice. But when I speak of silence silencing—of silence that happens as its own disclosure, I speak of no thing, of nothing. Silence silencing is not an attribute of anything and speaking of silence silencing might seem absurd. That sense of absurdity might well be due to discourses that have no sense for middle voice constructions such as the phrase *silence silencing*.[1] Or that sense of absurdity might be due to inclinations and predilections inherent in a language, a code of behavior, an enforced assortment of virtues, and what we ordinarily call rational good sense. Our dominant sensibilities can carry deeply ingrained traditions and lineages that function with enormous pre-reflective power to identify acceptable behaviors and beliefs and to conceal much that happens in and around societies. Our sensible rationalities in their good sense often cover over and ignore dimensions of living occurrences that happen (as it were) as no thing.

Michel Foucault's Sensibility

Foucault wrote in a sensibility attuned with the absence of life-defining divine power and of a unified, universal human consciousness. Meanings,

---

[1]. The middle voice formation I am using is intransitive. The subject, silence, does nothing in silencing. See Fragment Seventeen for additional discussion of the middle voice.

recognitions, values . . . all formations of discourse, awareness, and sensibility have lineages in which they (the formations) were formed. Those formative processes continue, but indefiniteness—silence, absence—infuses experiences of stability, relationships, dependability, and security. Solutions to problems are themselves problematic. For Foucault, the world is a site of thresholds in which creation, transformation, and dying seem perpetually accompanied by the silence of liminal indefiniteness. In that sensibility Foucault is interested more in problems than solutions, more in questions than definitive answers.

Although Nietzsche's "doctrines"[2] were not adopted by Foucault, Nietzsche's way of affirming free spiritedness is a friend to Foucault's sensibility. We found in Fragment Twelve that Nietzsche gave a name to beings who harbor chaos, who do not want to be thoroughly knowable, who affirm the silent excessiveness pervasive in their lives: he named them riddles and attempters, names that are themselves riddles. As he names them, he confesses that, far from definitive, the names are mere attempts, symptoms of his, Nietzsche's, yielding to the temptations of stable identities. As riddles, these beings, in the silent core of chaos in their souls, are beyond the subjection of ordering by names. In the dimension of silent chaos, they—the riddlers—happen beyond all order. Nietzsche's attempts to name them, seeming to call them to order by naming them . . . those attempts actually call into question his attempts to name them. His attempts undercut what he attempts to do when he names them free spirits and riddles. Chaos continues as nothing, as indeterminate silence in the lives of these beings, these so-called free spirits. Further, chaos does not happen as an opposite to order. Chaos is not disorder; nor is "it" formed in any sense. Chaos "happens" [as unorder] in the absence of anything.[3]

The First Question

The first question before us is: How I might speak to you of silence infused in the lively, bifurcated imagery of opposites? This imagery has immense power in our lives as we live together in common. I am speaking of silence *in* the bifurcating divisions that define our moralities and trustworthy knowledge, silence in the divisions that establish bases and frameworks

---

2. Self-overcoming, eternal return, transvaluation of values, and will to power.
3. See Fragment Fifteen, section "Sudden Sparks and Wonders of My Solitude."

for shared recognitions and feelings of normalcy, silence in the divisions that create clearly defined oppositions in the world we inhabit. I will call the silence in these divisions *breaches* that open in "fixed" realities and beyond them to the imaginary and thresholds of mere indeterminacy. Indeterminacy—silence silencing—*in* determinate formations.[4] I will speak to you in a manner that welcomes silence silencing. Speak in a way that turns us to silence and speak in a mood of affirmative astonishment that life happens with breaches that disclose no thing. In that effort I will tell you a story about three distinct occurrences in the imaginary of Western Europe, occurrences of . . . I will call it the *life* . . . the life of unreason. The story is a riff on aspects of Foucault's *The History of Madness*,[5] including the English, shortened version that bears the title *Madness and Civilization*. I tell that story with a sensibility quite different from one inclined to reverence, moral absolutes, and principled, transcendently grounded solutions to problems that arise in specific cultures.

With attention to the way Nietzsche riddled himself in the unorder of chaos, I turn to a part of Foucault's story of the inception of unreason, beginning with what he considered the essential thing when he is telling what we might consider a true story.

"The Essential Thing"

In Foucault's thought, the essential thing is not a thing at all. It is neither a truth nor anything definitive. Rather, the essential thing is the experience that a book or event evokes in readers or those undergoing an event. He says, "Now the fact is this experience [of reading his writings] is neither true nor false. And experience is always a fiction: it's *something that one fabricates oneself*, that doesn't exist before and will exist afterward" (Foucault

---

4. *Imaginary* in the context of this discussion does not mean "non-factual" or "merely a fantasy." We can understand it as a creative and symbolic dimension of the social world in which human beings create their way[s] of living together. Symbols can be extremely powerful in forming people's beliefs, values, judgments, and institutions. Indeed, people's beliefs, values, judgments, and the functions of institutions are part of a culture's imaginary. They are definitive in a society's ability to make sense of the world. Symbols are also dynamic and given to both minor and major changes.

5. I will also quote from *Madness and Civilization* (1973) when I find the translation preferable to the translation in *The History of Madness* (2006).

2001, 240). The essential thing happens as a book or event provokes people, moves them to have their own experiences in relation to what they read or undergo, incites them to have their own questions, their own actions and reactions. The essential thing is the individuals' fabricating—creating—due to the inciting, provoking, kindling that is provided by the writing or event. The essential thing is not *what* is incited, provoked, or kindled. It is people's creating—Foucault's words are *fabricating, experiencing*—in the impact of their encounter, their finding new directions in their lives, new possibilities, different ways of experiencing the world around them. Notice that Foucault, not unlike Nietzsche, has undercut the priority of truth and accuracy in his emphasis on fabrications. The essential thing is neither true nor false. "It" is beyond schemes of correctness and inaccuracy, about which I will say more. We may anticipate that what Foucault says about unreason establishes no lasting truths, that unreason feels like a powerful riddle, and that what is important in the part of his story that I riff on is one's ways of engaging protean unreason.

With the essential thing in mind, I turn to unreason's inception.

The Inception of Unreason

Foucault's story of unreason[6] in the Western imaginary begins with lepers, their excommunication and social outcasting by the Roman Catholic Church beginning in the eleventh century and extending to the early seventeenth century. The story begins with expulsion, banishment, and silencing of people perceived, because of their unhealable disease, as cursed by God, as dangerous sinners. Their outcasting, however, also bestowed on the victims the power of freedom from ecclesiastical and secular oversight.[7]

---

6. For Foucault, "unreason" is a floating term and not a stable concept. "Chaos" that Nietzsche speaks of and that I engage in Fragment Twelve, for example, functions in a way that "silence silencing" functions in this book. The fluid knowledge of Metis (see Fragment Nine), or the occurrence of a creation (see Fragment Eleven) are, as we shall see, "friends" of unreason. People might be more or less attuned to unreason in their sensibilities and the lineages that compose their sensibilities. For a more thorough account of unreason see Chapter Three of *Beyond Philosophy* (Tuana and Scott 2020, 71–107).

7. The leprosaria that emerged under the direction of priests and nuns curtailed "exilic freedom," although there were groups of lepers who formed their own communities outside cities and towns. In this narrative I draw heavily from Chapter Three of

A strange, complicating factor is that in their identity as outcasts whom God has cursed with leprosy as punishment for their sins, the lepers are also revelatory symbols of the mystery of God's grace: their lives are living witnesses to God's stern judgment of sin, but they are also blessed by God's promise of eternal salvation after they die. Condemnation and grace simultaneously. *Division* of the blessed and the cursed along with the division between the constrained and controlled Christian congregation on the one hand and, on the other, the exilic, often nomadic freedom of those lepers who are outside the jurisdiction and domination within the protection of city and church walls.[8] "Dearly beloved," a ritual from a church in Vienne states, "it has pleased God to afflict you with this disease, and the Lord is gracious for bringing punishment upon you for the evil that you have done in the world" (as quoted by Foucault). "The leper was then dragged out of the church by the priest and his acolytes *gressu retrograde* [walking backward] but he was assured that he was God's witness: 'however removed from the church and the company of saints, you are never separated from the grace of God. . . .' The lepers' salvation is assured by their exclusion: in a strange reversal quite opposed to merit and prayers, they are saved by the hand that is not offered" (Foucault 2006, 6).

Exiled with cursed freedom, many of the lepers were nomads beyond the power of established authorities. They were silenced by the power of the traditional doctrines and practices that required their exile, and at the same time they were seen as recipients of the revelatory power that God bestowed upon them as living testimonials to God's punishing judgment of sin. They were condemned with salvific grace, "saved by the hand that is not offered." In the combinations of such contraries as cursed and blessed or silenced and revelatory, we find the germination of unreason. We find undefined absence, a silent lack of similarity, in the between that connects the differences. The silent lack, this undefined absence, breaches the divisions, breaks the connections of specific and opposed differences. Mere silent absence both adheres to the differential divisions of, for example, exclusion and inclusion—breaches the connections of

---

Beyond Philosophy (2020, 85).

8. "The word *division* in the present context names a dynamic form of social practice that separates people on the basis of spiritual/moral/physical qualities—separates the clearly virtuous and normal from those perceived as deviant, law-breaking, anti-social, or abnormal" (Tuana and Scott 2020, 86).

the opposed differences—and silently opens out to nothing in particular. I will say more about breaches.

Instilling Tenebrous Unreason

I continue to riff on several parts of Foucault's work in *The History of Madness* as I move now to the seventeenth century. The Crusades have ceased, and leprosy has begun to fade in Western Europe. The aspect of Foucault's account that I emphasize as I make this move is silent division—division, for example, between the condemned and the blessed—combined with exclusion and exile from the company of the saints and from the city's community. The power of what is known as rationality is growing. In the division between irrationality and rationality, rationality is assumed to be the stable basis for propriety and truth; in the division between punishable deviations from normal virtue and laudable social normality, normality is presupposed as acceptable and right. Irrationality should be excluded from the Commonwealth by rational authority and practice, and abnormality should be corrected or excluded from the community of upstanding citizens. The pressing issue in this sort of division, combined with exclusion and exile, becomes one of finding ways to carry out the exclusions, deciding how to segregate and sequester whatever or whomever violates or challenges proper rationality and behavior, how to exile from day-to-day social life those who are social deviants.

Unreason, however, as Foucault finds it in the seventeenth century's imaginary, is not within the circumscription of the divisions of rationality and irrationality or the divisions of virtuous propriety and moral deviance. *Unreason* does not mean *irrational*. Rather, unreason is sensed as outside the order that makes possible the bifurcation of reason and irrationality. Unreason began to be sensed vaguely, not as the opposite of reason but as a hovering and utterly corrupting difference beyond the bifurcations of reason-irrationality or moral rectitude-moral degeneracy.

A sense of shadowy unreason emerged in the seventeenth century as secular rationality began in many areas of communal life to replace scripture and church as the single agency of authoritative knowledge and truth. Although leprosy receded in Western Europe, a growing sense of a different kind of danger, like the danger of something demonic and evil, emerged in shadowy dimensions of people's minds. This difference was experienced in the nonrational strangeness of dreams, especially in the terror of nightmares, or in the ways hell was presented in paintings, sermons, and scripture—a misery of suffering bodies and souls, an unorder of agony unlimited by time, the graceless underside of God's forgiving hand. Unreason in this era appeared also in ecstatic sexual passion and in gasps of panic and fear when death—surely it is death—like a shade silently passes by or visits your child in the darkness of night. In this imaginary, reason does not define or control that indefinite and frightening utter difference. Rather, unreason's tenebrous occurrence is both outside the jurisdiction of reason and goodness and happens as a subverting, completely different quasi-absence *in* reason's and goodness's connecting divisions: unreason interrupts the divisions between reason and irrationality, and between goodness and badness (or evil). We can use nonwords when speaking of this phantasmic, utterly silent, threatening chimera that infests these divisions: unorder, unsense, unlaw. Unreason, a menacing sort of madness in the world that puts in question not only the authority of law and order, morality, and good sense but also breaks the serenity of their differences—the differences of law and order from disorder, the differences of moral goodness from badness, and differences of rational good sense from irrationality and nonsense. As awareness of unreason gained power in the imaginary of that era, the seamless and ordered opposition of the bifurcated pairs—rationality and irrationality, law and disorder, goodness and badness—was shaken, not shaken by options but by the shadowy uncertainty and doubt invested by unreason at the very core of the rationality that made the bifurcations sensible.

Unreason, silently, vaporously drifting; mere silence in rationality's texture seemed to pervade vaguely the pairings, excessive to the divisions themselves, thus corrupting the atmosphere that seemed to hold the promise of certainty, sovereignty, and the sanity of well-ordered rationality. Unreason breached the divisions. Gapped them, we might say. In this imaginary, the breaching stuck to the divisions, haunting them like a nightmare that will not go away, and seemed to allow unprotected exposure to silence silencing, to unorder in the order. It interrupted the rationality of the opposition of reason and nonsense like a breach in a dam that restrains water as water pours through it. Reason's opposing difference to senseless irrationality harboring no reason at all? Goodness and badness breached by complete absence of values? Goodness and badness breached by nothing? Law and disorder breached by chaos? Breaching that seemed to drain substantive life from reasonable differences and to permeate the mortality of the breached?

The breaching seemed like—felt like—a silent supernatural attack that threatened the authority of reasonable order as reason gained enough power to form its supreme rule in the secular order of knowledge and conduct without reliance on supernatural power like God's grace. Unreason, however, provided no substantial beings, such as lepers, by whose sinful, exiled bodies and souls could be held in the light of salvation, and God's order could be reaffirmed with rituals of confession, forgiveness, praise, and adoration. With the sense of unreason's intrusive breaching, reason, virtue, and social order seemed alone in their challenged authority, alone with silence silencing and without power to erase or exile the sticky adherence of unnatural unreason, unorder, unlaw.

In the imaginary of that time people felt a need for something to unloosen unreason, carry unreason away, exclude it from the community, render it powerless by its sequestration. In this felt dilemma, attention turned to those people who were obviously not rationally or morally directed beings. They should be clearly recognized, rationally named, categorized, and sequestered. In this domain that was within reason's power, the domain of secular power over abnormal, mentally afflicted, diseased, deviant, dishonest, violent, unchristian people, Foucault found a region of descent that in its lineages stretched back to the exiling of lepers. The authorities exiled and deposited a mélange of socially deviant people in various types of containment structures (including those that were once leprosaria), in dungeons, and in what would come to be known as hospitals. Confinement in these places would surely banish the scourge of unreason that some people embodied and vividly revealed, take away the scourge that cast a pall of danger and doubt on the society, perhaps heal some of them, and restore the healed to the rightful order of their given nature. They were confined for the sake of purifying the community, hidden if not healed, literally out of sight and hopefully out of mind.

But unreason in the imaginary of the period was not subject to healing or sequestration in its breaching unorder. Shadowy senses of unreason continued to plague lives for whom so much mattered, plague them by the breach "where" nothing mattered. While sensible and virtuous people, in the name of reasonable justice, subjected assemblages of human beings to exilic confinement with the cruelty only humans can visit upon each other in order to maintain organizations of goodness and truth, the sense of unreason nonetheless stuck to the imposed divisions, opening crevasses of unconfirming silence in the midst of measures taken to eliminate the breaching silence. Those breached divisions yielded senseless thresholds opening out to indeterminate expanse where spiritual nomads could become riddlers who give birth to creations unimaginable in the imaginary of unquestioned decency and verity.

Foucault is tracing lineages of practices such as outcasting, deporting, secluding, categorizing, healing, and normalizing, to name a few. These lineages are not dead forms of past practices. They are lively in people's inclinations and disinclinations, in imaginary formations, and in the sense we make of the world around us. Many of the given predispositions in people's lives function pre-reflectively and are beyond individuals' control. They compose our minds—our sensibilities—as dynamic traditions, habitual patterns of behavior and recognition that can merge with other traditions and habitual patterns of behavior and recognition. During the seventeenth, eighteenth, and nineteenth centuries pre-reflective figurations in the Western imaginary carried with them senses of physical (leprosy) and spiritual (sin) illness vaguely attached to exiling practices. Those senses and practices that disclosed God's immeasurable grace mutated with new and forceful images of reason's immeasurable ability to disclose the secrets of the world, to authorize people's proper behavior, and to define human nature. Yet the shadow of unreason diffused and darkened rational light and held open dimensions of life whose darkness revealed the absurdity of the exaggerated claims for universal rational truths and authority. We can say with a smile that unreason is a constant companion with the imagery of sovereign reason and the idea that the world is essentially reasonable. Unreason seems to allow sovereign reason to appear, if ever so ominously, as the absurd artifice that it is.

Authoritative knowledge began to change with the impact of the natural sciences and specialized knowledge in the eighteenth and nineteenth centuries. Institutions transformed, and imaginary forms, such as senses and ideas of human goodness that guided social progress began to emerge. Such senses and ideas were quite distinct from those that carried so much power in the "Age of Reason." The sense of unreason also shifted in the transforming imaginary. Instead of hovering obscurely in bifurcating opposites *outside* of reason and normal virtue, unreason seemed now to permeate reason and virtue themselves. For some people, unreason appeared silently to infuse and to expose reason to *unform*, to an unending emptiness in the plenty of rational power.[9] The foundations of Truth and Goodness began to tremble in this emerging sensibility. Authority as such was in question. For those people who felt a draw to the collapse of the authority of rational good sense, unreason appeared to open the way to the freedom offered in silence. For some, the rising complex of senses and feelings seemed like an opening to mystery that beckoned them to fluid pathways of uncertainty, to thresholds seeming to verge on chaos, to verge on nothing. Mystery in the breach, we might say.

This turn of mind led some artists and philosophers to affirm the chaos of silence silencing, gave some people pause with a sense of God's absence and reason's inadequacy in the face of dimensions of reality where no words entered. Different plateaus of perception developed, and new vistas opened out. Unreason, far from a menacing quasi-presence, seemed more affiliated with indeterminate opportunities for thought and composition, an opening out to what Nietzsche riddled as free spiritedness.

In this turning in the culture's imaginary, a feeling of mystery thus occasionally replaced anxiety in the interlacing of nothing with the things of the world. In a sense of mystery, what is taken to be true knowledge might well seem truncated, a bit foolish in the exaggerations of its claims, shot through with local interests and absurd assumptions—that, for example, "life" has a fundamental purpose, that all countries should have one kind of government, that bumps on a skull predict mental and behavioral traits. In the force a sense of mystery can have, good ways of life might seem not so good—class structures, for example, wealthy lives indifferent to those without wealth, or lives ordered toward eternal happiness by sacrificing the interests of one's own self. In the indefinite and infusing power of breaching silence silencing, unreason might seem more like a call than a curse, and new vistas for thought and artistic creation could emerge with the astonishment engendered in renewed life, a vivacious sense that welcomes the dangerous life of exilic spirituality.

---

9. The unsettling of Reason's sovereignty happened in many ways. I have in mind, for example, in addition to Nietzsche and Søren Kierkegaard, such diverse thinkers as David Hume, the later Friedrich Gottlieb Fichte, Denis Diderot, Friedrich W. J. Schelling, Jean-Jacques Rousseau, William James, and George Santayana. Among the many threshold artists are Claude Monet, Vincent van Gogh, Pablo Picasso, Frida Kahlo, and Diego Rivera.

As I turn from hovering unreason in the Western European imaginary of the seventeenth, eighteenth, and early nineteenth centuries, I want to note sensibilities that are attuned to dimensions of reality that are obscured or ignored in the canons of acceptable, academic rationality. I am speaking primarily of thinking that often seems nonsensical to "normal" good sense, that is usually considered at best wrongheaded, at worst silly drivel.[10] Nietzsche and Foucault, for example, wrote in a sensibility attuned to the draw of ways of thinking that emerged in the impact of unreason's power in Western imaginaries. They felt the need for a different kind of knowledge and judgment in comparison with the intellectual canons they inherited. They often found certainties and established identities that were problematic and questionable, ambiguous and doubtful at best in spite of seeming "literal" clarity. Unreason's silent breaching within the divisions between rational and irrational, between good and bad now could seem to have spread to the cores of rationality and morality. Without reason or value, unreason, as some people began to feel it, breached rationalities, good sense, and irrationalities. *What* is bifurcated as well as the bifurcating *divisions* are breached by silence silencing. The bifurcations could seem to be reasonable and unreasonable at the same time. Reason and good sense as well as the bifurcations between opposites seemed to constitute thresholds to indeterminate mystery unbounded by any formation.

Mere exposure of unreason in the serious endeavors to establish with overwhelming power enduring states and institutions of Right and Authority explodes the notion of universal Reason. The exposure of unreason explodes the possibility of totally rational consciousness and moral duty, explodes the force of the imagery of the priority of subjective consciousness. Unreason's *breach* in the dream of Reason, its opening in mere silence silencing, in the difference of nothing at all, can interrupt the authority of a society's rationality and normalcy, qualify it, disrupt its play of sovereignty. In the strange, anomalous power of this displacement

---

10. Søren Kierkegaard, Friedrich Nietzsche, Martin Heidegger, and the entirety of "postmodern thought" are typical examples of thinkers and ways of thinking that are considered by some British and American "schools of philosophy" as non-philosophers. Early in my career I was told by senior colleagues that not only were Kierkegaard and Nietzsche not philosophers, but that Hegel was also not a "real" philosopher. As recently as two years ago, a senior philosophy major who had taken only analytically oriented courses before he took my course on Nietzsche said at the end of the semester, "I think Nietzsche is crazy. I mean, really crazy." He was referring to Nietzsche's thought, not to the time after Nietzsche's breakdown (when he did not write at all).

an individual's sensibilities can shift; people can begin to sense the incompleteness that accompanies their own ways of composing, thinking, and living; a feeling of riddling goes with the person's identifiable presence, a feeling of porosity and unease, perhaps unease in the silent incompleteness of rational formations of certainty.

In summary: In Foucault's story, the germination of unreason in the Western imaginary happened as lepers became the site, as it were, of a division that made their random, contagious, and incurable disease understandable—the division between sinners punished by God and the obedient congregation of the church. The division joined differences in the context of faith that provided at that time the basis of reasonable clarity and recognition: sin coupled with punishment and grace, physical disease interconnected with spiritual transgression, the presence of eternal and paternal Power intersected with mortals, with finite spiritual children in constant need of guidance, discipline, and forgiveness. Exile from the congregation and the city came to be defining factors in this Christian rationality that formed the recognition of lepers as people who should be excluded from the company of those "saved" by their obedience and spiritual health. The cultural "genes" that developed in the practice of exiling began to make exclusion and exile sensible—reasonable—when behavior or belief obviously and habitually deviated from rational good sense. Over the course of three centuries rationally conceived institutions replaced both the exilic nomadic freedom of lepers and lazar houses as spaces for exclusion and exile. Reason was king of the secular realm as a sense of "something" unsayable, uncapturable, obscurely present emerged, something that seemed to hover strangely beyond the reach of rational grasp. Odd people, thieves, mentally ill people—all those whose behavior deviated or opposed rational good sense in the communities where they lived, not entirely unlike sinners in a congregation of the blessed, captured in the power of reason whose authority defined the world—these star-crossed, often wicked people carried with them the unreason that infected them, carried it into rationally constructed spaces that separated them from the citizenry and in the process became defined by Reason. But that grand project did not work. Unreason breached the very bifurcations of good and bad, rational and irrational, normal and abnormal. It increasingly seemed to open thresholds of indeterminate nothing, a non-dwelling region for spiritual nomads. As imaginaries changed, the breaching of bifurcations—the "infection" of no thing in the connections among things—became apparent, not only in bifurcations but also *in* reason itself. Whereas in the seventeenth century an eternal, unlimited God functioned to save the souls of condemned lepers, in the eighteenth and nineteenth centuries a sense of limitless nothing began to emerge and to occasion freedom—dangerous freedom—for exploration and fabrication with those who became attuned to "it." Unreason—silence silencing—dismantled the authoritative sovereignty of reason by doing nothing. That sovereignty began to seem absurd to some people, to seem to make apparent *un*reason at the core of monarchical Reason. Unreason—the mere absence of reason—began to inspire ways of thinking and creating as a much-altered sensibility became possible in the crumbling of what was named the Modern Era.

Silence, Silence Silencing, Sticky Silence

When I use the word *silence*, I often have in mind a formed situation that is characterized by silence. Silence is identified by the formation: the silence *in* a room, the silence *in* a prairie, silence *in* an event in a life. When I use the phrase *silence silencing*, I refer solely to silence's . . . happening. I studder at this point because of the awkwardness of saying "I refer solely to nothing happening." The "happening" of silence "is" nothing, no thing. Silence "is" not the same as the form that identifies "it." A formed, identified silence occurs with no formation (such as a room, a prairie, or an individual). Rather, the "happening" of a formed silence "is" complete silence. Silence without a "where" as a silence happens where it is. Mere absence in a presence. No thing in something characterized by silence. The awkward distinction means kinds of silence in formed situations—silence in the room or the prairie, for example—"are" mere nothing pervading the room or prairie, infusing that prairie and whatever is in it.

Sticky silence refers to a silence and silence silencing "happening" simultaneously, like when unreason breaches the reasonable—defined—separation of factors that people see as opposites.[11] The breach intersperses the formed division of opposites and puts the reasonable certainty of the division in question. The breach pervades the division's felt rational

---

11. I am using the odd phrase of "sticky silence" with a smile. "Sticky silence" is nonsense and cancels itself: silence silencing is nothing, and the words' self-cancelation is their performance. The phrase enacts its own meaninglessness. Or I could say that sticky silence means that nothing happens in silence silencing's adherence with a silence.

stability; it silently gaps the division in sheer unformed silence silencing, in *indeterminate* silence silencing in the determination of the differences. Attunements with the breach might open the possibility of degrees of difference as distinct to an image of atomistic opposition. Or we could say, in attunement with silent unreason, the differences of good and bad might seem viscous and unfixed in their meaning. It's as though the breach incites a storm of possible unordered images, values, meanings, and figurations of power; and in this real imaginary's tempest, sticky silence adheres to the tremors and convolutions that shake carefully constructed foundations and give images and meanings to infuse and mutate. The breached divisions might seem to leave stable rationality and morality excluded and exiled—a nonrational reversal with neither condemnation nor approval. With, perhaps, riddled free spiritedness for a questionable shelter.

I began this fragment with the reminder that many systems of belief, sensibility, and discourse cover over and ignore dimensions of living occurrences that happen as no thing. Why would that concealing happen? Maybe the question should be, why wouldn't the concealing happen? Civilization depends on human lives with inherent spiritual and ethical inclinations that are universal, doesn't it? Otherwise, power, not the value of human lives, rules. Conquest and domination, not equality and compassion, establish laws, values, and hierarchies of importance and privilege. Without universal values and meanings based in human nature the future of humanity might seem hopeless. There would be nothing transcendent to appeal to when societies are structured by oppression, exploitation, and brutality. Human lives then could be owned and exchanged for other commodities. People would be lost in a sea of struggle for safety, satisfaction of basic needs, and as much power as they can win to control what happens in their living space.

I believe that the images of life composed by struggles for power and survival without Meaning and with only volatile, mortal meanings as sources for spiritual life are profoundly disturbing in many if not most Western imaginaries. This kind of disturbance, this kind of feeling, motivates people to cover over the threat of silence silencing's breaching, to cover over dimensions of no thing imagined as infesting every aspect of human lives. It—this kind of disturbance—is, I believe, a prime motivator for affirmation of stable foundations and universally obligatory values.

Countless people also have been and are profoundly disturbed by the possibility of lives infused with nothing and ending in nothing more than mortal memories in addition to the influences and impacts they had on other people, institutions, and communities. "No ultimate reward for my service to God and my efforts to obey His will?" someone might say. "No reward for the moral goodness I have tried so hard to cultivate? You're telling me that my mother vanished completely when she died? She 'lives' only in memories and influences in other lives, in lives that are themselves totally mortal, earth-born, and sublunary? She 'lives' only in lives that are not her? She still *feels* alive to me. I know she sees me, that she lives in some way I don't understand. I feel her presence. And you tell me that when her earthly body became a corpse nothing was left of *her*? Only silence silencing? No soul? No eternal spirit? No Greater Being that she became a part of? I think you are a fool! Worse. You are a damned fool!"

I believe that the fear and anxiety incited by the possibility of no Meaning and by silence silencing are evident in the recorded history of Homo sapiens. They—fear and anxiety—gave rise to all manner of rituals and sacrifices and to castes of special people—seers, for example, who divine the past and foresee the future and priests of many kinds who preside over rituals and sacrifices and know the will of the Gods. But living in a world without Gods populating another present but hidden world? Without divinely gifted mediators between Gods and people? Without revelations of Gods' wills and desires, and with no more life for the dead . . . nothing . . . no godly answer for those who mourn? No formations independent of human inventions and situations to give site and meaning to silence? Silence silencing in the boundaries of lives? Our lives wouldn't make any sense, would they!? Or at least they would make sense only in the imaginaries of Homo sapiens, in our astonishing ability to make worlds of Meaning and memories that linger to form lineages, lineages that conceive minds that, strangest of all, are able to imagine themselves in the vastness of silence silencing.

FRAGMENT SEVENTEEN

Silent Space

"In the vastness of silence silencing." *Vastness* can suggest something of very great size, something enormous like a mountain range, an ocean, or a desert. Closer to its Latin origins, however, *vast* can also suggest empty and immense, boundless.[1] *Vast* in the sense of empty suggests absence of boundaries that provide formation and identity. In that suggestion, the noun, *vast*, would name immense space and not a thing.

"Sticky silence," we have seen, names the adherence of silence silencing with a specific silence. A silence and silence silencing happen simultaneously. The descriptive thought about simultaneity here is complementary with the descriptive thought that silence accompanies sounds—all kinds of sound—just as silence silencing accompanies a silence in all kinds of formations. Stated another way, bounded silence may adhere to unbounded vastness in silence silencing.

An implication of this language and imagery is that a continuous edge happens in the simultaneity of a silence and silence silencing. A specific silence, the silence of a desert, for example, or the silence of a life's moment, is on a verge as the individuality of a silence seems to fade in a person's awareness, seems to slip into vast silence silencing. An individual is on a brink of boundlessness, on a continuous yet porous edge, an in-securing verge with the individual's secured and limited space.[2] As sounds

---

1. The Latin word *vastus* means empty, deserted, wasted, unoccupied. I use the word *vast* with emphasis on "empty."
2. Verge has a rich history. I am using the word in its sense of outermost edge where a particular formation is at its extreme limit and verges on a limitless expanse—a

yield to silence in people's experience, as noise fades and quiet silently emerges, an awareness might also emerge that is not a conceptualization within the strictures of good sense and reasonable boundaries. Rather, a person might become aware in silence silencing, aware in the verge of empty vastness, as identity seems silently to fade into nowhere, aware in the presence of a silence slipping silently into nothing. Happening here, now. In that awareness people might well experience a sense of lostness combined with wonder. Quietly amazed in silent wonder and nothing.

Do the words I am using sound too positive, too wonderstruck? People experience in countless ways a silent in-securing verge within secured and limited spaces. Many of those experiences accompany trauma and shock. I have known many people who lived through traumatic, life-altering experiences. Sexual abuse or rape, experiences in war, deaths of those they loved, destruction of their homes by fire, wind, or water.

I knew a young man whose wife was killed in a car crash on their way to a honeymoon vacation. A few hours after their marriage, her lifeless body lay at his side in the demolished car, lay silently in the midst of shouting, lights flashing, sirens . . . his world and his self seemed to slip through a crack split open by . . . by . . . he couldn't remember exactly by what. But his world and his self nonetheless seemed to slip away into dizzying, empty silence. He was not seriously injured. I came to know him a few weeks after the wreck. When I spoke with him, he seemed to be "holding it together," as he said. He wanted to continue his plans to go to college. He enrolled as a freshman and had a dorm room. But what he could not hold, the utter silence that separated him from her and from himself as he knew himself, was too much. When he was by himself and started to read something or to think about anything, or when he wanted only to sleep, his trauma took over and he slipped into silent emptiness that seemed worldless and timeless.

My neighbor several decades ago suffered with PTSD after the Normandy landing and two and a half years of active combat. He was a friendly person, a loving father and husband. But he would lose his sense of time and place on the Fourth of July when fireworks began to pop and

---

silence, for example, verging on the infinite excess of its limit, silence silencing. (In the sixteenth century, *verge* named a region under the authority and control of someone. The word at that time could also mean the rod or staff that symbolized the authority of its bearer. Another of its early, now obsolete meanings was penis.) See also David Farrell Krell (1990), *On Memory, Remembrance, and Writing: On the Verge.*

boom and rockets exploded with fire in the air. He would walk aimlessly for hours without knowing where he was. He would speak to no one. His wife said it was like he left himself and someone else was there. He was frightened, angry, and abusive. He woke up sweating with terrifying nightmares. In the language I am using, his disorder was something like a silent gap, a broken connection. In the gap's silence, I believe, when in his hometown he heard explosive sounds reverberating in the distance, he saw images of shattered dead bodies piled on dead bodies, felt the unspeakable, silent terror in the killings . . . the killing after killing after killing. He walked lost in horror and depression, as though he were on the brink of nothing.

    A woman I knew said she left herself, felt like she was floating above herself, when she was a child and her father forced sex on her body. She lived a silent gap in her own presence. Mere nothing seemed between "her" and the body somewhere down there. Living her absence as it silently happened, she found her child's world, a world where she could smile and tell Dilli, her dolly, about adventures they would have in a place only she knew, a secret place where the trees talk and everyone is kind. She was close to forty when she told me about her experience. Occasionally, she said, she still felt haunted by her child's world when she was flooded by memories of her father's smell and the sounds of his grunting as he moved inside her. Those memories combined with her sense of levitating, her sense of hovering in her airy sanctuary. In those moments she would not know who she was or where she was. She was aware then, I believe, in a haunting verge of undefined space.

    These people were similarly aware in their trauma of what we might casually call uncertainty, uncertainty not only of their identities but also of their lives. They experienced uncertainty *in* the space of their lives, angst beyond language and conceptualization in the broken continuity of themselves, in their awareness as they verged on the absence of themselves. I believe they were aware beyond anything they could say. The happening of absence in their living presence, not only the absence of a person or some being, but the feeling of mere absence. Feeling absence before one could think of "mystery" or "inconceivable." Some people speak of looking into a verging abyss in their lives without picturing themselves standing on the edge of anything. They simply experience "abyss," silent space without borders. Absence in their defined space. Verging vastness. No images.

    I too have experienced traumatic events and verging abyssal absence. In that awareness I had nothing really to say for months. Not much even when I talked about what happened or merely about what to have for dinner or how cold the weather is. In addition to the literal meaning of what I said and heard . . . a sense of silent emptiness filled the hollows of my mindbody. Nothing there. Nothing wonderful about those experiences. But they did give me to wonder as my awareness slid on the verge to nothing at all, to wonder as feelings of meaning lost their energy, as though there were a leak to nowhere that left only silent gaps, silent gaping in silence, staring as colors faded and mornings were misery. Why? Not a robust why. A life-tired one. Empty wondering without wonder.

Depressions can have their own prospects, their own ways of opening out to the way things are when our "normal" lenses and senses weaken or shut down. Empty buckets in an almost colorless world. "Foul morning when light pierces darkness" is the first line in a poem by a college friend. Depression lets *unheimlich* space, unhomelike space, happen without the illusions of rainbows, moonlight, and shades of color. Sunlit brightness fades. The light of the world fades. Silent nothing. Nothing matters.

Unheimlich space. Silent space between words, for example. Silent space with vast prairies. Sky-space. Empty space. Unhome space we might say awkwardly. *Unheimlich* space gains meaning when people tarry or remain in a place for a while, when they dwell . . . and "there" becomes "here." But when you find a place of previous dwelling gone, as you stand there looking, listening, and remembering, you might feel an emptiness that was there even when you were at the dwelling place with its defined rooms, its sounds in other rooms, its smells from the kitchen, the crises that seemed so important in their moments. You might feel in its absence how precarious the dwelling place was, feel as though the fullness of dwelling there were porous, as though *unheimlich* space silently indwelled the dwelling. Perhaps another building stands there, where your dwelling place stood, now with other new buildings that make a strangely different environment and wipe out any trace of where you lived and considered "the home place." Perhaps as you look you have a sense of *unheimlich* space spacing without care, without meaning. Silent space that is far more apparent to depressed awareness and the awareness of those who have acute experiences of loss and trauma than to people with joy in their lives or to people in their "normal," everyday interactions.

It's not that *unheimlich* space does something silently in a space of dwelling. Space beyond form doesn't do anything. The world, the world that we indwell and that indwells us, is where spaces of meaning form in their many intensities. The figurations of space that we inhabit together as people with identities . . . let's call them life-spaces in the figurations of which we spend the times of our lives, spaces where all sorts of new things, new lives, emerge and pass away. They are areas of creation, death, feeling, conquest, and so much more. Life-spaces constitute room for emotions that can shrink as the power of meanings weakens or intensifies with affirmations, hopes, and loves. When the power of meanings diminishes, a person can feel more acutely the verge of empty space in the spaces of their lives. In that sense of extremity humans might feel both anxiety and astonishment as they contemplate life on the edge of nothing. Contemplation with wonder that it, contemplation, is happening. People can be astonished *in* the happening as contemplation reverts to itself, reflects itself, on the fringe of itself in the silent spaces of lives.

I turn now to attend to silent space from a quite different angle and prospect, the space of the birth of new images (that are real). Consider imagination's creative power through Hippolyta's words:

> The poet's eye, in a fine frenzy rolling
> Doth glance from heaven to earth, from earth to heaven;
> And as imagination bodies forth
> The forms of things unknown, the poet's pen
> Turns them to shapes, and gives to airy nothing
> A local habitation and a name.[3]

"Gives to airy nothing / A local habitation and a name." "Airy nothing," a name for mere space, undefined space, spacious nothing. Emptiness and not a substance. Not a thing . . . the space in which imagination with a poet's frenzied eye bodies forth the forms of things unknown. The space of creation verges immediately in the poet's awareness, Hippolyta seems to say, verges immediately in the poet's "fine frenzy"—in the poet's madness of moving outside the strictures of normal existence, the madness of *ek-stasis* when one's senses rise and hover at that boundary where what is speakable fades out to vastness beyond speech and thought and, so it seems, "doth glance from heaven to earth, from earth to heaven" in a process of invagination, a folding in of heaven and earth that turns vastness into a boundary and becomes a cavity with nothing-yet-said, a cavity of airy nothing that is well disposed to the poet's pen. The cavity, a harbinger of earthlyheavenly contingency as the poet's pen turns nothing-yet-said into

---

3. William Shakespeare, *A Midsummer Night's Dream*, act V, scene 1, lines 12–18.

shapes, shapes that do not erase airy nothing. Rather, *with* the cavity the poet's pen gives to airy nothing a local habitation and a name as the diaphanous glimmer of airy nothing infuses the existing shapes as they enter the verge of the world.

In the cavity, the space of airy nothing suffuses the poietic shapes as imagination silently conceives them. Whatever is child to the poet's *ek-static* imagination carries with it the chaotic invagination of, in Hippolyta's metaphors, heaven *and* earth.

I experience wonder as I feel airy nothing . . . silent aether-like nothing . . . verging on the habitation bestowed by imagination—airy nothing seeming silently to hover while disappearing, undulant like ghosts in the shapes' appearing. Wonder that something comes with nothing in . . . I want to say "in the robust delicacy" of the spaces that host the births of images. Images that are real, that are *really* images. Images that do not dissolve into the airy nothing that silently permeates them and their spaces, but rather images that body forth in grand imaginaries. These imaginaries invest (or infest) already persisting formations. Altogether they comprise a silent mélange of formations, a disordered cosmos of orders with uncountable incompatibilities and empty spaces, a chaos of knowledges, uncertainties, and desires. I experience wonder as I feel the chaos of arising and dissolving orders of feelings and forms, as I write in astonishment as though I am following a dancing star and give those who read these words to wonder whether what they read is true, whether the generated images and the words they yield are even real enough for us to consider their entry into a space of credibility.

In our turn to wonder, robust delicacy, uncertainty, persisting formations, and desires, what of love in the silent cavity of airy nothing? I am turning to the ambiance in people's lives when a love silently finds forms of expression, when, we might say, a love takes place. I am turning to the porous soul of deep loving that can permeate people's being and transform them silently. I am turning to guiding moods in people's lives that form a dimension where their most heartfelt longings and senses of fulfillment happen . . . silently. This ambiance is a site of profound inner experiences, an interplay of energies, a bodysoul that touches everywhere in a person's sensibility without congealing into any identity. I want to set aside the deep, restless longing when people experience the absence of something important in their lives. That longing might be dreamlike, like a dream for my life that has not awakened in the undreamed world but that silently is also haunted by a feeling of emptiness and restlessness, a persistent sense of something missing. That kind of longing composes a sort of soul-sickness. I want, rather, to speak of loving in the present context of silent space.

This region . . . this silent bodysoul dimension is so elusive and insubstantial! If you have ventured there in your alertness and allowed its affective disclosure in your life, you probably can sense how others live this quiet insubstantial depth where amorphous moods happen—desperation, despair, or unfocused disappointment, for example. Or a pervasive sense of heart-felt determination in spite of unfavorable odds and troubled waters. Or, if you have experienced devoted love, you are probably able to sense devoted love's happening in the depths of another's soul.

But how does devoted love happen, happen silently in the dimension of bodysoul? Happen not in the transcendent force of cosmic nature or as a divine gift, but as a creation in the cavity of airy nothing? I do not have in mind the time of "honeymoon love"—"first love"—which is so richly (and often so beautifully) endowed with fiery desire for another and laced generously by airy nothing. I am thinking of heartfelt, committed love that originates silently and without warranty, without guidance by good sense, without aim or goal beyond itself. Devoted love is a way of feeling from which "reason" can take its cues, but the feeling of love takes its cues from the love itself. Its constancy in life-spaces requires reaffirmation, requires, we might say, love's return in its devotion from itself to itself, or it will lose its depth, its intensity, and slip away. In its rejuvenations it is like a renewing conception, a genesis that happens again and again. Its beginnings do not stop. Love's devotion—its silent constancy—is love-made in the cavity of airy nothing as it bodies forth in decisions, attention, concern, support, and delight in the beloved's beauty beheld in the lover's eyes. In the cavity of airy nothing, love's constancy is ever becoming and is always on the verge of silently falling away.

In that verge the feeling of love guides the lover to a way of living, motivated by a spreading, inclining, silent desire to be always *yes* to the beloved's life, a desire to live opening out to the loved other—to open with the other before the other is other—desire to feel the other's being where the other is and is not other,to feel the other's living before the fixation of images and judgments, to have the strength to be without defense and exposed to the loved one. The soul of love is silent and hushes sounds that attempt to describe it. This does imply, doesn't it, that I need to hush!

Wonder, despair, grief, spiritual dying, creativity, desire to be, hatred, joy, devoted love—all on the verge of vast silence silencing in a cavity of airy nothing. So much space suffused with silence pervading the lives in it.

FRAGMENT EIGHTEEN

Touching Silence[1]

Anne

I had never held a girl's hand in a movie theater. Not even Betty's when we walked from her house to town on our first date ever and watched a Saturday afternoon's cowboy movie at the State Theater. We were in the seventh grade. I would go over to her house now and then to play with her younger brother in order to be closer to her. A year later Betty and her family moved away. We still viewed ourselves as boy-and-girl friends up to the time she left. But I never touched her skin, and I never saw or heard from her again.

    A big change happened when I sat next to Anne in the Key Theater three years later. The Key left the cowboy and wolfman movies to the State and Pix Theaters. It had big time Hollywood movies and actors like *A Kiss in the Dark* with actors like Jane Wyman and David Nevin or *In the Good Old Summertime* with Judy Garland and Van Johnson. I have no idea what Anne and I were watching, but I do remember where we were sitting as we watched the screen and that I was scared. I had no idea what Anne thought about me. But I really liked her. For a while—a long while, about half of the movie—I shifted my body slowly toward her for the sake of a good angle so that I could easily—without the people sitting behind us noticing—touch her hand that rested on the arm of the chair. I was trembling when in an act of anxious bravery I put my hand on hers. She turned her hand and closed it enough to hold mine. It was warm and

---

1. In this fragment I will limit the discussion to touching between people.

soft. Holding her hand holding mine was *so* different from the untouching distance of just sitting beside each other. We looked straight ahead, holding hands—feeling hands—until the movie was over and lights came on. We went across the street to the drug store and had a coke together. Being with her there, sipping and talking, felt different from when I sat beside her before I touched her hand. Even though she was on one side of the booth and I on the other, the distance seemed changed. I would say now that it was infused by the particular experience of herskintouchingmyskin. We seemed closer than we were as we sat beside each other before we held hands. I knew her now in a different way.

Touching as Anne and I held hands, feeling her skin feeling mine, triggered something inarticulable in me. Put me on a path leading out of my dreaming innocence, one that I had not been on before, leading me in a direction that previously I could not have imagined. I would say now that holding hands with Anne birthed a new feeling, a silent attunement in our touch, a silent touch of intimacy in the midst of the theater's shadowy darkness, among the sounds coming from the screen, in the heart of the hormonal chaos of early adolescence.[2] I believe the experience of holding hands with Anne on that now-so-distant Saturday afternoon played a role in setting a direction that led to my recent discovery: I want to write about touching silence.

I am writing about skin silently touching skin? Really? Skin is an organ. The body's largest organ. Yet it doesn't see, hear, or talk. It is not the agent of smelling. It certainly does not think. Its sensation is feeling. Skin feels heat and cold, pain, pleasure, vibrations, and much more. Rather than the neurological formations and abilities of skin, however, I

---

2. I do not speak here of the erotic aspect of Anne's and my holding hands, because at this moment in the discussion I want to focus on the immediacy of touch and not on the elaborated meanings of a touch in various situations, not on the sexual implications a person might find in a touch, for example. The difference between the feeling immediacy of touching and an elaborated reflection on the experience of the touching plays an important role in this fragment. In my "dreaming innocence," this, my first experience of holding hands romantically with a girl, was metamorphic; something latent in me became actual, and a quiet transformation began to happen. A new sensitivity began to arise. I have taken the phrase, dreaming innocence, from *Either/Or*, Volume 1 by Søren Kierkegaard (1987). He uses it to describe the first stage in the development of distinct and stirring erotic emotions. The young individual feels hazy attraction but not full-fledged erotic desire. This attraction is a feeling of closeness as one is "gently rocked by an unaccountable inner emotion," "an intimated desire" (1987, 76–77).

am focused on how skin-touching-skin composes a silent, pre-reflective touch-world of its own.

When Anne's and my hands touched and held each other in the Key Theater, so many meanings and mores came into play. Touching only hands as we did meant affection, not "I love you," but "I like you," "I want to touch you," "I want you to touch me." It meant innocence and sensual pleasure and excitement. For us, the hands-together was a very long way from touching lips. If one or both of us had gloves on, the experience would have felt different . . . it would have *been* different in the absence of herskinmyskintouching.

If one of our skin's colors were perceived as not-White, if it had been seen as Black, for example, in that small Oklahoma town, Wewoka, in the 1940s, our touching hands would have carried complicated and dangerous meanings. With Anne and me it was *White* skin touching *White* skin. Different-colored hands touching each other like Anne's and mine touched would have been judged as outrageous, and it would have been perceived as outrageous in part because touching composes a dimension *beyond* meanings and colors. It happens, I said, as its own world. There is nothing like it. Skintouchingskin is intimate in its silent immediacy.[3] The intimacy of touching in a racist environment, touching with its dimension of happening beyond meanings and colors, intimates the racial mixing that is forbidden in the dominant mores of such a society. The dominant sensibility mediates and gives meaning to the touching. If you ignored the meaning of color and you, White, and the other, Black, held hands, especially in the shadows of a darkened theater, you would defy that very powerful moral code as your bodies in touching travel beyond the code's strictures, in the silence of skin-feeling-skin as your touch and the other's touch return each to the other. The returning happens, not as I touch you and then you touch me. There is no "and then." Touchingyoutouchingme is without mediation. Touching happens silently without reflection or the reflective noise of categories or counting. You might *look at* the touching as you touch. You might *think about* what it means as touching happens beyond thought or sight. You might *categorize* it. You might *intend* to touch as you touch. But that's not at all the same as touching.

---

3. When skin touches another's skin violently, as in a fistfight or otherwise hurting another, the touching is a violation, an invasion, an incursion. I am limiting the discussion to touching without violation, the touching that soothes or puts another at ease even though the touch is unexpected and, perhaps, hardly noticed reflectively.

Something happens in touching: the touch, the sensation, the feeling . . . a silent infusing presence that revolves on itself without reflection. Touching. Mutual feeling. With Anne that time in the theater, gentle touching. For me then, a wonderful sufficiency in its moment. I remember it still in its virginal innocence. Holding Anne's hand felt like all I ever wanted. Enough in the touching. Dreaming innocence.

"A silent infusing presence that revolves on itself without reflection," I said. Touching happens pre-reflectively in the sense that it happens independently and without the mediation of other types of consciousness. Many different motivations can incline a person to touch another person. But regardless of motivation or interpretation, touching *in its* very happening is neither an acting subject nor a receiving object. I think of it as an infusing immediacy. I intended to touch Anne. But the touching is not the same as an intention to touch. In touch, skins silently come together. Skinwithskin—blind, deaf, dumb, without taste or smell, without conceptual structure—touching happens as its own sensation, its own physical awareness. Touching is where one and another, apart in their presence, silently infuse, blend in-touch.

◆ ◆ ◆

A Short Excursus about Immediate Awareness

Throughout this fragment I speak of immediate awareness. The Indo-European base of the word aware is *wer-* and has the connotations of alert caution and vigilance, to be or become aware, to be wary, to keep safe, to protect. A night watch, for example, on guard at the fringe of a military encampment might feel wary when, in the dark, he hears a slight cracking sound coming from a nearby, deeply shadowed copse, or when the hair on the back of his neck stands up for no clear reason. Such wariness is feeling *in* an unpredictable situation of potential danger. Rather than reflective consciousness about his situation, the guard has a sense that arises *in* his situation; the guard feels a possibility of harmful presence. It is a sense of unspecified precarity. The feeling is immediate in the guard's situation.

If I say, however, that the guard's feeling is *about* his situation, if I say he is aware *of* his situation, in contrast to immediate awareness, the situation is an object of his consciousness. The guard realizes that he is frightened and is able to make a judgment about how he should react and what he should do. This realization and response are conscious (or I could say *aware*) and reflective. In the phrase "he is aware of his situation," "of" has an objectifying function: "situation" is the object of the preposition, "of." When, however, I say "a sense of unspecified precarity," sense is not mediated by reflective consciousness and is not an object. "Of" functions in this usage as a subjective genitive and indicates an immediate feeling that the guard undergoes and bears.

When I use the phrase, "awareness *of* touching," "of" functions as a subjective genitive. "Touching" in this phrasing serves as a gerund (a verb used as a noun) that retains its verbal meaning in its nominal function: "touching" means an event of being aware *in* the event of touching. In the phrase, awareness of touching, "touching" is not an object of "awareness" (awareness does not possess touching) nor an object of "of." I am speaking of immediate awareness, awareness that is not mediated by objectifying consciousness, awareness that one bears in the touching.

◆ ◆ ◆

Feeling Nothing?

I have touched dead bodies. My touch then reached a dead end. Touching the skin of the dead in its immediacy felt strange to me, uncanny. The skin of the dead happened, sort of. Not at all like skin of the living. Skin of the dead is not unnatural or unearthly; it happens belonging to a corpse, not to an alive body. Touching a corpse's skin is not more silent than touching a living body's skin. Touching the dead's skin happens with mere cold silence. No quickness in its feel. Is that what it's like to touch something *with* nothing? Skin of the dead is not nothing, but in that touching no-life is returned. Nothing alive there with skin of the dead. As I touched my mother's cadaver, I remembered her touch when I was a child, the warmth of her cheek when she hugged me, the touch of her hand on my hand at night, the touch of her lips on my forehead. I remembered how her skin felt as I held her wrinkled, bony hand during the time of her severe dementia. Her skin felt alive in our touching fusion. Fusing in touching, her hand gripped mine in wordless recognition as she slowly raised her head and her misty, faded blue eyes turned to me. A month later, touching her dead body shocked my memory, my imagination. The absence of *her presence* in my memory and imagination regarding her were different from her absence in the corpse's skin. *In* memory, images of her connect with other images. The interplaying images are alive as images. But touching her corpse? My living feeling *in* the touch happened without living resonance . . . with neither living presence nor image. Unfeeling silence. Like a living moment with silent nothing nowhere. Dead skin. Silence . . . only silence.

Attentive Awareness in Touching Silence

Nancy and I have striking clocks in our house.[4] Sometimes, when I am concentrating on what I am reading or writing or when I am almost asleep, I become aware of the chimes just after they stop. I heard them but I wasn't paying attention to them. Were there ten or eleven? If I am listening carefully to someone in a conversation or when I am concentrating intently on something I am reading, I don't hear the chimes at all. I become oblivious to what is happening around me. I believe this kind of experience is common in everyday life: focused attention on something in particular can affect inattentiveness to the place, time, and circumstances in which the concentration occurs. On the other hand, I believe that while people have many responses to touching, mindfulness *with* skin-touchingskin is rare. By "mindfulness," in the context of this discussion, I mean undisturbed attention *in* the happening of silent skintouchingskin, *in* the feeling of touching silence. Not attention *on* who is touching me, but attention *in* the touching moment. For that attentiveness to happen, I need to be calm and undistracted. I need to be alert in the happening. Intellection is not helpful in this sort of alertness. Immediate awareness *in* touching silence is not a happening of intellect or an object of intellect.

"Immediate awareness *in* touching silence" means in this context immediate sensing—feeling-immediacy, affective, non-observational awareness. That awareness does not carry over, does not translate into something intelligible. We can certainly talk about it, as I am now. We can describe it as simultaneously immediate and aware. We can identify the affects of touching. But alertness to the happening of touching silence does not require intellectual activity. It requires attentiveness that allows a person to be attuned to touching silence in touching awareness.

---

4. Nancy Tuana, my wife.

The feeling of touching silence happens in-between the ones who touch.[5] Skintouchingskin does not take place like two people who each touch the other so that each is a subject of an action and also the object of an action. Conjunctive actions do take place as one touches the other, but *in* the touching something else happens that is meant by the dash in the word *in-between*. Individuality remains as non-individual infusion happens—Anne and I are different individuals before, during, and after holding hands. But the happening of touching is neither the one nor the other. Touching is silent permeation, physically coming together in-between. Touching is its own feeling, beyond identity, quite silent in its non-subjective, non-objective awareness. It's a strange awareness in our English language's conceptual world, a world that is ordered primarily by the dichotomous formations of subjects, verbs, and objects.

To be alert in this awareness, however, I need my mind to quiet, to mind *in* the touching in-between, to let the touching be foremost in my mind, heeding it in *its* happening. I am able then to be mindful in the touching, mindful in the mind's quiet feeling *in* skinwithskin.

TOUCHING DIFFERENCES

I was twenty-two in September of 1957, just graduated with a BA and a Fulbright Fellowship to study philosophy in Germany, and on a ship sailing from New York to Bremerhaven. The passengers included a large number of Fulbright Fellows. Paul Freeman was one of the Fulbrighters on his way to Berlin to continue his training as a symphonic conductor. My wife, Donna, a White woman, and I formed a friendship with Paul and his wife Cornelia, a pianist. It was our first friendship with Black people. On the twelve-day voyage we frequently ate at the same table and after dinner enjoyed dancing to the music of a six-piece band. We occasionally changed partners—Paul with Donna, I with Cornelia. Donna came from the deep South, Memphis, Tennessee, and I from a small Oklahoma town where Blacks and Whites never mixed socially. On that ship, the *MS Berlin*, Donna and I had our first experiences of touching Black skin in a context of friendship and equality.

Experiences in the United States of the huge, imposed differences between Black and White people in the context of brutal racism silently faded. We came to be at ease with each other. At least Donna and I felt at

---

5. I speak of two people and not more for the sake of simplicity.

ease. Paul and Cornelia seemed at ease. We four talked openly about racial issues. But I would not presume to say that I know what they might have felt and kept to themselves. The dancingtouching, I believe, played a large part in creating that ease. Cheek to cheek now and then, handinhand in addition to feeling each other's clothed bodies, silent feeling-immediacy surpassing inherited formations of judgment and identity. The "in-" of in-between . . . that infusion happened along with the individuality of our styles of dancing, with the contents of our conversations, with the power of our different life-histories—*that* something more—that intimacy that silently happens in touching happened with us.

I was happy in my experience with Paul and Cornelia. I wonder now why I wasn't shocked, stunned by that silent immediacy. I believe the strikingly different environment of the *MS Berlin* had a considerable impact on my sensibilities. I was literally at sea with a diverse group of people from many different countries in a strange water-world. I heard languages I had not heard before, ate new foods, enjoyed having my first taste of alcohol, ever! I saw dolphins breaking the water and racing the ship. At night the sky was often like a silent sidereal baldachin in its star-filled vastness that diminished and elevated us at once without a hint of light in the darkness that surrounded us. Always, I felt waves rolling the ship on the vast spread of sea. I was in unfamiliar surroundings, both immanent and remote, different from any I had known. I felt a new sense of freedom, a sense that I was in a threshold that in its outstretching, indeterminate, unfixed opening carried . . . was it a promise of transformation? I was a long way from the town of Wewoka that I knew as home. Dancing with a Black pianist, shaking hands with a Black symphonic conductor, hugging him, he hugging me; kissing her cheek, she kissing mine when we went our separate ways—all that seemed like part of a sea-change, "rich and strange," nothing of "coral" or "pearls" or "sea-nymphs" or, hopefully, "full-fathom five," but a sea-change nonetheless already begun on the *MS Berlin* in the indeterminacy of a future before which I stood on the rocking ship.[6]

Touching Paul and Cornelia touching me opened a new world beyond any where I had been. That opening seemed consonant with the flowing world I was experiencing, a water-world that felt nowhere in particular but a water-world in which I moved on a floating speck in an expanse that seemed boundless with silent openness everywhere.

---

6. The term *sea-change* and the quoted words are from Ariel's song in Shakespeare's *The Tempest*, Act 1, Scene 2.

I believe that silent openness everywhere resonated deeply with touching silence, the feeling in touch without identity or color or judgment.[7]

---

7. Donna and I and Paul and Cornelia visited together both in Germany and in the United States while we were in graduate school and before we settled in different parts of the country.

FRAGMENT NINETEEN

Moments

Opening her mind and imagination gave joy to her heart.

Planting Rhododendrons[1]

I remember one afternoon in my yard as I prepared a place for planting rhododendrons. I remember the ground was hard with clay, that I had to integrate compost, peat moss, some fine wood bark, and a bit of crushed eggshell into it. I intended to nurture the plants, to let them grow by providing the minerals and moisture they needed. Digging and sweating in the afternoon's sun, I was aware of the day's warm brightness. In its silent shinning I sensed the vast space behind my back and beyond the trees. "The stretch of silent shine," I remember thinking.

I wanted the rhododendron flowers in spring to break the spell of winter, to recall in their burgeoning a time of rebirth and in cloudy, chilly March to forecast days of warm brightness. I wanted their blossoms to renew a sense of budding life. With my hands in the dirt and mulching it into garden softness I remembered . . . I silently *felt* my family's agrarian past. For a few moments I could see my grandfather in overalls and a floppy hat behind a one-horse plow, the sun's heat streaming down as

---

1. For an earlier reflection on planting rhododendrons, see my book *The Time of Memory* (1999), 280–81.

he struggled to hold the plow in place as he cut furrows into the almost black earth. I felt closeness with the earth and with him as I kneaded the clay with the mulch. Not like the closeness I might feel with a poem or music or a way of thinking but closeness *in* the silent feel of dirt on my hands, under my fingernails.

As I minded the earth in my hands, the reddish clay turning toward dark brown, "ashes to ashes, dust to dust" flitted through my mind. Earth to earth?, I wondered. Life and death? I didn't "really" know why I was able to plant something that would grow. I knew some of the scientific reasons why plants could grow, but botany can take you only so far. Earth to earth, dust to dust? Dirt is alive and nourishes the lives of plants. Plants nourish the lives of animals and people. "Dead" plants, as they return to earth, nourish it . . . the dead bringing life to the earth. Will my ashes silently nourish earth? Nourish the sea? My hands in the earth . . . "the stretch of shine" all around me . . . silent questions arising and taking me beyond the circumference of my intelligence. I sensed how far, how invisibly distant, how silently my feelings carried me: back to the living of the now dead; silent images fading while the silent feelings remain . . . for a while. My silent imagining forming me for moments before the moments silently deform as I worked the silent earth. Imaginary formations that, almost like shadows, dimmed away. Silence to silence. Are these images like earth? So many things that remain in the earth decompose, lose form. Images of things fade . . . like wisps of things in the earth, as the soundless images decompose. The differential distance separating earth and imagination seems, mirage-like, to transpose, to become a gauzy space of likeness in the disappearance of the forms they harbor. They—images and earthen-forms—seem almost to touch each other, hovering close as they seem to melt away. Hovering, silent distance. Images melting away leaving silence as though they never happened.

I knew that each handful of dirt contained millions of organisms, cells, sub-cells, infinitely small things, and traces of things. The worm in the dirt would seem gigantic in comparison. And *I* was thinking and feeling these things in the silent space of my imagination. I felt strange in this flow of thinkingfeelingsimages, I with my hands in the dirt, my eyes shining as I looked up, reflecting the shine of vast and formless cosmic space on this sunny day here with the earth.

I felt strange in my memory of "dirt farming" as I dug in the earth to plant rhododendrons in a city's suburb, strange in belonging here, strange in the sense of wonder I felt in my awareness of my home and of not belonging completely here at my home. At that moment I felt the silence in imagining, the silence in the earth, the silence of my grandfather as I imagined him. The silence of my home's *Unheimlichkeit*, my home's uncanny strangeness in my home's familiarity. It all felt so weird. It all felt so real.

Earth *to* earth. Image *to* image. Dust *to* dust. Ashes *to* ashes. Am I somehow connected with each "to?" Are the "to's" like a flowing river, a flowing river that I am? From images, with images, to images? Am I, the one with the images, the one who remembers in the richness of images . . . am I the one who harbors images, who bears their fading, bears the disappearance of the images . . . am I an ashbin? A silent grave?

Am I the silence before the image, the silence of the image, the silence after the image? Nothing that I remember or imagine is there beyond the remembering images. I feel the silence in the "to's," in prepositions on the way to nowhere.

Pausing at 3:00 a.m.

I would like to call on your imagination for a moment as a passageway to the next moment of awareness.

Imagine sitting at 3:00 a.m. on a concrete bloc . . .
    amid a pile of rubble . . .
        in the remains of a city . . .
            that has been bombed.

In the light of a bright moon, you can see the shattered remains of buildings and streets stretch out before you.

No one is around . . .
    Silence. Dead silence.

Can you quiet yourself? Still yourself? Open yourself to silence silencing in stillness? Silence to silence without words? Without thoughts? Without meaning? Can you feel silence silencing?

Can you imagine simply opening yourself to the remains of destruction for a while? Sitting on the concrete block amid a pile of rubble . . .
    without an interpretation?
    without judgment?
            Just stillness and silence silencing

Silence beyond Imagery

The 3:00 a.m. imagery provides a moment to occasion awareness with silence silencing—with nothing—in the midst of disaster. Quiet. Destruction with earthly silence, with silence silencing without meaning. I find strange opening myself to silence silencing—letting silence silencing—without imaginative formations in my awareness. Focusing on and with imaginative formations and paying no heed to silence with the formations seem "normal" to me. But imageless silence with disaster or with something beautiful (stars or a painting or a body or a field with falling snow) or with an afternoon's pause in the midst of my work . . . awareness in undisturbed, imageless silence is not so normal. At least not for me.

Silent absence comes with imaginary formations, whether they be thoughts about some thing, memories of what happened yesterday or years ago, or images of unicorns. Imaginary formations happen in the absence of the imagined event or thing—*in* the absence, *in* the silence. Imagining happens without the presence of the imagined events and things. It seems immersed in absence: the reality of images with the silent absence of the imagined. But that reality is not always disconnected from the non-imaged event or thing. As I talk with someone who is frowning, I imagine her when she is smiling. When I see a friend for the first time in many years, I imagine him when he looked younger. I see a housing project on the site where I remember playing softball—so many of the events and things in our lives are interlaced with silent absence, even when they seem so totally there. As I write now about experiences of silent absence, I am not only attempting to make sense of it. I am also writing with awareness in it.

Awareness in Senseless Silence.

Hello, sun in my face.

Mary Oliver

I sat several years ago close to the Atlantic Ocean, looking eastward with an image of the coming sunrise. In the falling darkness clouds heralded the unrisen sun, clouds tinted crimson, burgundy, magenta, fading pink—a mirage of colors spreading across the sky. The sounds of the rolling waves coming to shore intensified the silence of the sky, of the colors, of the moments between shoring waves. The image I have is of the sun seeming to rise out of the ocean, a ball of flame, not soft light like the moon's beguiling, gift-like glow, but a blazing inferno that can sear my eyes, burn my skin, and also let me see, not images of the sun, but lighted things freed in their lighted presence from the cover of night.

Brightening light. Lifting darkness. Enflamed clouds auguring. . . . Then . . . . A thin crescent. . . . A rounding brightening sliver rises seemingly from the sea, rises hugely and quickly, dimming to nothing my images of a sunrise.

THE RISING SUN.

Rising in blinding silence. Coming up from the sea. I look away as I . . . not hear, but as I see, feel the brilliant . . . blinding . . . shining . . . silent sun.

THERE.

Only later do I feel grateful to the images that led me to my place looking eastward, a place now in the sun's hot glow. The images' fading out—decomposing—came with the loss of what they held in mind and in the presence of what no mind could hold.

The Storm and the Moon

Last night I saw the full moon. After two days and nights of violent, earth-shaking thunderstorms. But these were not merely thunderstorms. They were

THUNDERINGLIGHTNINGCRASHINGSTORMS

Dark, tumbling, speeding clouds, icy hail, pouring water like an angry empyrean river. Lightening flashing around dark yards, fields, highways, streets with seemingly immediate, crashing, rolling thunder. Flooding streams and rivers. Cars rolling in rushing water. Homeless under-the-bridge people running for their lives (two didn't make it). I rely on your imagination and memory to communicate what the storm was like.

In the lightningthundering there were no images for a moment. Not in the ligthtningthundering immediacy. Sky-opening streaks flashing crashing rumbling. . . . You know what I mean . . . when a storm is so powerful, TOO THERE to be imagined. Yes, I was seeing the flashing, hearing the thundering. And yes, seeing and hearing are senses. In that sensing what I saw and heard were images. The images were not themselves the thundering and lightning. They were the sensing of the thundering and lightning, sensing in thunder thundering as forks of lightning flashed, seeming to crack the sky, sensing experienced *in* the thundering and lightning that seemed to overwhelm silence for a fragile, ephemeral moment, passing away silently in the silence that never left them.

That was yesterday and the day before.

Last night in stary-bright, blue-black darkness a full moon rose in a cloudless sky. A breeze stirred branches of oak trees, sweetgums, sugar locusts that silently cast long, quivering shadows on the grassy earth. The silent shadowed earth, too, seemed to waver with the moving shades, moving without human meaning, untrue to the forms that interrupt the moonlight. A dog barked far away. The engine of a distant car. Moonlight . . . utterly silent . . . glowing everywhere. Except where the light shined on things that make shadows. Dark, silent shadows of houses, a chair on a porch, corn stalks in fields, copses filled with silhouettes waving like seagrass in disturbed water. A tall building far away, appearing as a dim fantasy with its shadow wafting out to roofs, to a spire, as distant and insubstantial as a quavering vision. The silent, undulant moon shadows, dark shapes filtering through forests and cities . . . moon shadows holding the night. Moonlight and shadows flowing together in darkness, silence silencing everywhere.

Treacherous Mentor

"*In the great silence.*—Here is the sea; here we can forget the city. True enough, the bells are still noisily tolling their Ave Maria—it is that lugubrious and foolish yet sweet sound at the crossroads of day and night— but it lasts only a moment! Now all is silent! The sea lies there, pale and shimmering, and cannot speak. The sky puts on its evening mime, forever mute, with red, yellow, and green colors, and cannot speak. The low-lying cliffs and the rows of boulders that march into the sea as though in order to find the place that is loneliest, none of them can speak. The vast taciturnity that suddenly befalls us is beautiful and terrifying, our hearts swell with it. . . . It grows even quieter, and once again my heart swells: it is terrified by a new truth, for *it too cannot speak*. . . . Speech, and even thought, are despicable to me: do I not hear behind every word of mine the raucous laughter of error, hallucination, and the spirit of delusion? . . . Oh, sea! Oh, eventide! You are treacherous mentors! You instruct human beings to cease being human! Should they give in to you? Should they become as you are now, pale, shimmering, mute, monstrous, resting contentedly on themselves? Elevated sublimely out beyond themselves?"[2]

In Fragment Three I spoke of Connie's walk in a diminished forest of ancient trees. These trees "seemed the very power of silence, and yet a vital presence." She finds liveliness—"a *vital presence*"—in the trees, in their "unspeaking reticence," their "sustaining reserve," their "kinship with whatever lives out of itself." She found among these trees what was thoroughly absent in the cities: she found the very power of silence with vital presence. In the silence of the trees' intense inwardness, they were connected sublimely beyond themselves, connected with other lives in the silent power of their own lives.

I emphasized the words *vital presence,* vital presence that accompanies the power of silence beyond speech, beyond thought, beyond human. Vital presence that, in Connie's words, is the power of the trees' lives, the power they embody with silent dignity and reserve. In this vital presence they are akin to whatever lives out of itself, akin to the sea and its own unspeaking reserve, akin to the sky in its silent, boundless expanse. I also had in mind, when I emphasized *vital presence,* the mentoring that Nietzsche speaks of, the vast taciturnity of the pale and shimmering sea and of eventide as light silently falls amidst many, so many colors in the earth's coming darkness—I had in mind the instruction of human beings by this vast taciturnity, a mentoring that encourages a deep, silent desire in human souls to stretch out beyond themselves and their humanity in the power of *their* lives toward a vital sublimity. "Elevated sublimely out beyond themselves and their humanity."

This mentoring is treacherous for humans. In its silent power, treacherous mentoring of human beings encourages processes of self-overcoming, a transformation of lives that moves them toward . . . not toward a family of humankind . . . but toward the silent power of beings, like the power of the trees Connie found on her walk. Unspeaking trees that reticently, silently live beyond the bounds of human imagination. Treacherous mentoring that encourages a growing sense of kinship with the sea and earth and sky, with low-lying cliffs, kinship with boulders tending down toward

---

2. Friedrich Nietzsche, *Daybreak,* number 423 (1997).

the ocean's watery. . . . Not an ocean's grave. Rather, an ocean's moving, living depths where boulders rest quietly in themselves in the deep sea's vital, silent presence.

Strange, isn't it? Alikeness of humans and boulders and trees? Alike in being alive. Alike in the animated intensity of silence's vital power beyond language and thought. Alike in the power of silence. In the power of being alive that, mentor-like, guides people away from noisy, intrusive, distracting cities and lugubrious Ave Marias, guides them beyond the enclosures of speech and thought, and guides them beyond their human identity to the silence, "the great silence," in being alive.

FRAGMENT TWENTY

A Story of Silent Unreason

Nomadic Freedom with Imagination's Dangerous Instability

Distortion: Tell It like It Is.[1]

In Fragment Thirteen I told a story about unreason with primary attention to silent breaches in the bifurcations of opposites, the silent breaches in such sensible divisions as blessed and cursed, right and wrong, good and bad, rational and irrational. Now I want to tell a story about unreason with primary attention to silent nomadic freedom and imagination's dangerous instability.

Nomadic freedom and unstable imagination became increasingly manifest in the lineages of expulsion. Those lineages silently infested the growing authority of secular, rational sensibilities that inclined people to find ways to extract undesirable people from their society. These lineages constituted, not rebellion or refusal of rational sensibilities, but absence of reason in reasonable efforts to establish sensible and normal communities. This is a story of the power invested in what is known as reasonable good sense as people struggled to purify their human environments by ridding themselves of those individuals who seemed to live in the absence of rational, moral sensibility. Surely the most reasonable way to pursue such purification is to put depraved, defiled, and dissolute individuals in reasonably defined and constructed institutions. Not lazar houses (leprosy had virtually disappeared), but sensibly conceived exilic buildings that confined dangerous deviants and protected the good folks from those

---

1. Phrasing by Nancy Tuana.

deviants with their spiritual and physical illnesses. In the telling, I will repeat some information that is available in Fragment Thirteen as I give this Fragment its own independence.

The Story's Lineages

This story of unreason, like many other stories, is conceived in silence with imagination and imagination's freedom from reason's authority.[2]

The story begins with people suffering from leprosy, begins not with concepts or truths but with victims of leprosy's bacteria, bacteria likely brought to Europe from the Holy Land in the twelfth century.[3] At that time people could easily imagine the incurable disease as a sign of God's punishing judgment. The Church, as the institutional incarnation of God's will, is the worldly agent for carrying out the divine, loving condemnation. Lepers were condemned by the very flesh of God's body, by the redeemed congregations of blessed people led by the spiritual progeny of the apostles' touch.[4] The excommunication took place ritually in churches, graced houses of good repute where unreason's forebearers were conceived and born. The names of these ancestors of unreason are excommunication, exile, expulsion, and excision. The "ex" in their names in this story suggests "power," power to remove, to name, to separate out.[5] Unreason belongs to a linage of power-formations that emerged with the excommunication and expulsion of lepers. God's authority provided stability for the righteousness of the action. Stable truths, authority vouched safe by accepted structures of power such as the Church and later by secular

---

2. This Fragment is based on Michel Foucault's genealogical account of the formation of the insane asylum in *The History of Madness* (2006). In that account he coined the word *unreason*. I have lifted out (extracted, you might say) those parts relevant to the reasonunreason fusion. As the story unfolds, I hope you will begin to feel the intense silence of unreason, a haunting silence accompanying an unquestioned rationality. From some angles of imagining unreason, haunting silence is a phrase synonymous with unreason.

3. Fragment Seven began where we are now beginning, but with a different agenda and emphasis.

4. The reference is to apostolic succession, the uninterrupted transmission of spiritual authority from the apostles through successive popes and bishops, a doctrine taught by the Roman Catholic Church.

5. Later "ex" also suggested power to restrict, educate, judge, and normalize.

authorities such as governing aristocrats, doctors, and experts in various fields are in unreason's lineage. Also in the lineage were the strange powers of the exiles' nomadic freedom and its unsanctioned silence. Freedom and silence were nestled in the imagery that developed regarding lepers. The imagery formed an unconscious imaginary of those "ex-ed" people, an imaginary often accompanied by whispery feelings of indeterminate danger, of foul diseases and homelessness, unlicensed desires—not quite sexual but feelings nonetheless that could cause people to tighten unwittingly their genitalia and relish the imagery of spiritual stability that would allow them to feel secure with hope for purity and joy.

Another element nestled in this lineage was a sense of imagination's dangerous instability, its nomadic space and lack of an overarching, unimagined order, its indifference to God's Truth as God's Truth was known. Universal, earthly orders must not be indebted to imaginative formations, indeed such "realities" as God's gift of life and His plan for human lives must be protected from imagination and its indifference to truth and security in people's lives. This lineage was a witches' brew populated by a contravening, disordering mixture of factors that did not bode well for the seamless Truth of Christianity or the tidiness of rational logics.

The Imagery and Power of Reason

By the sixteenth century, reasonable people could be certain that the universe is good and God or deified Reason is its ruler. Unreason's lineage carried images of reason as stable (also stabilized) secular reason. Secular reason "bodied forth" in worldly institutions, laws, and values while the Church's authority faded in the light of unsanctified, authoritative rationality and morality. They—secular rationality and morality—began to replace the Church's haloed authority with the authority of civil institutions and systems of principles and values founded in unquestioned sensibilities and social mores. Those systems established the validity or invalidity of what was said and done; and by the sixteenth century they began to function as the standard for what is proper, for what is established based on the rational dominion of the universe, and for what is *really* true and good and just. But deep in the hollows of rational certainty and outside the jurisdiction of rational comforts and systems of images—silence, mere absence, nothing at all, silent and indeterminate thresholds in the heart of reason's formulated stability.

The imagery of reason also harbored deep within its rationality the lineage of inclusion-joined-by-exclusion. Confining and silencing (forced inclusion) the excluded—the incurably ill and the violators of rational-moral good sense—in reasonably conceived shelters became the name of the game. Many lepers had lost their exilic, nomadic freedom as they were gathered and involuntarily held in facilities called lazar houses. What to do with the lazar houses when leprosy suddenly declined sharply in most of Europe in the sixteenth century and there were no expelled lepers on the horizon to give promise to those houses? They were like empty concepts waiting for content! But the obviously immoral and dangerous people with venereal diseases who should not live with decent healthy folks? Aha! These ill-fated, sexually diseased people became the excised captives in emptied lazar houses. In time, these kinds of facilities increased in number as "houses" that were imagined and erected by wholesome authorities and became the vessels, not only of sexually diseased people but of those unreasonable people—the immoral and mad people. The "unreasonable," "criminal," "immoral," "diseased," "mad": these people came to be held together in silent exile *within* the monuments to reason and goodness. These housed, silenced deviants came to include the destitute, a wide range of crazy people, homosexuals, harlots, thieves, the heavily indebted . . . anyone who chronically strayed from proper, ethical, or rational behavior. Such behavior is without reason's sensible and moral guidance and is reasonably exiled in governmental quasi-prisons in which, in spite of the good sense embodied by these houses, good sense and firm reason did not hold sway. Rather than reason, bedlam, disorder, mayhem, disease prevailed.

◆ ◆ ◆

A Short Excursus

We will see that unreason can play a vitally important role in societies. Its domestication is a foolish project—the more foolish for all the projects' seeming successes. In this kind of domestication, enormous energy is dedicated to the formation of institutions, knowledge, and practices that . . . *stubbornly* is not quite the right word here . . . densely and ignorantly attempt to kill unreason as though unreason were some thing that could be killed, attempt to silence and disempower "it" by the forces of normal coherence and systems of stable conceptualization, to silence silent unreason. These attempts yielded rational formations on island-like kingdoms of Truth surrounded by a tumultuous sea pounding their shores, eroding their perimeters, a sea with profound subterranean creatures in its impenetrable dark. Reason is so very limited in its range of sense. It is so often unreasonable in its self-assessments. Dangerous in its confidence. So unaware of its deep-seated kinship with its own absence, with unreason and mere silence that accompany the careful formulations.[6]

◆ ◆ ◆

Contagion and Disorder in Reasonable Formations

Now with an *absence* of reason oddly in attendance, the image of reasonably conceived shelters for these people, conceived with rational good sense to protect the commonwealth, began broadly to interfuse with the occluded imaginary of nomadic freedom, unsanctioned silence, disease, and unregulated imagination. These sensibly conceived harbors for the unfit began to appear not only to protect the good folks but also appear as centers of sickness and immorality, unhealable contagions that might seep through the cracks and fissures of those shelters. They—the shelters—awakened in communities situated close to them fragments of ancient myths, vaguely shadowed by transcendentally tinted evil. They incited a sense, at first only whispered behind closed doors, that those odious retention houses shelter and exhale foul vapers out of their chimneys and cracks in walls and floors. There must be a force, perhaps satanic, certainly silent, at war with fair decency and life-giving Truth, a force now infested *within* the walls that define reasonable attempts, if not to purify, to reasonably contain a legion of indecent people. Unreasonable anxiety bordering on obsession with unprincipled, non-moral deviations from acceptable citizenship permeated the citizens' imaginations. Deep anxiety arose, especially in darkness, often formed in dreams as specters—as quivering shades—rose in the dark-like vapors from the chimneys and sewers of the buildings of containment. Imagination must be harnessed, trained, and educated to

---

6. This paragraph is modified from *Beyond Philosophy* (2020), 90.

renounce its unreasonable freedom, its figures that arise out of "the airy nothing" that is often the womb of images previously undreamed. Reason's primary weapon? Objectification. But I am getting ahead of the story.[7]

◆ ◆ ◆

The Emergence of Silent Unreason with Reason

I would mislead you if I gave you a well-structured narrative about unreason's emergence. Unreason's story comes in broken pieces and without defining form. Its fragmented lineages and formlessness are part of the story. Unreason is so insubstantial that its very name is a red herring that guides us away from the patchy fragments that compose the narrative: unreason is not a single thing and has no defining logic. We have seen that the lineages were formed first by divisions (exclusion, exile, etc.) within the protection of God's grace. The leper is judged and abandoned by God and is at the same time promised eternal life in heaven (according to the Church's ritual of expulsion). Michel Foucault's phrase is "the (lepers) are saved by the hand that is not offered" (2006, 85). The ecclesial setting for the interfused differences of division (from the Church) and inclusion (in the Church's redeemed gift of salvation)—differences of division and inclusion interfused *in* the lepers' holy excision—will not last. The formation of division-from-and-inclusion-in, on the other hand, emerged as part of a dynamic and defining structure of power that had authority to prescribe what is true and good. It is a formation that will endure through several centuries before what Foucault calls *unreason* makes present its unreasonable, sometimes haunting, always silent absence.

"Makes present its unreasonable, sometimes haunting, always silent absence." "Totally absurd," you respond? Yes. Yes indeed. I am writing about the death of reason's and good sense's unquestioned authority. About the vested, rupturing silence pervading frameworks of assurance that promise their unbreachable and lasting endurance. I am writing about nothing at the core of values and beliefs, an opening to the possibility of creativity, an opening to deviation and distortion in relation to "acceptable" thought and art. Unreason enjoys kinship, as it were, with madness and the babble

---

7. The two quoted phrases are from Hippolyta's song in Shakespeare's *A Midsummer Night's Dream*, act V, scene 1, lines 12–18.

of insane people. Unreason also composes an opening for new ways of thinking and writing, for artistic styles that were inconceivable before the eighteenth and nineteenth centuries. I will come back to this point.

In retrospect we can say that unreason, in addition to the sense of contagion I pointed to in the previous section, is foreshadowed by behaviors like those noted above, foreshadowed by people whose conduct and affect seemed to indicate an absence of reason—not irrationality but no reason at all. These people were identified within such social structures as networks of truths and morals, families, schools, and accepted means of communication. They threatened the authority of these structures by their distortions, deviations, and distractions within the structures, by their senselessness, their illnesses, their danger to others, and most importantly by the imagined possibility that they bore witness to something—or Some Thing—beyond reason's control.

We have seen that the buildings in which these deviants were collected and exiled resurrected images of seeping contagion, contagion of bodies covered with pus-filled sores, certainly, but also those who spoke without order, bodies that frequently lost control of themselves in paralytic or epileptic seizures, people who had apocalyptic visions of the Coming Final Days. These exiles, excised from society as they were, housed together like a vile decoction of unorder that breathed silent, poisonous vapors into streets and byways, gardens and homes, filling the air like an invisible curse as it suffocated infants at night, caused stillbirths, and spread an invisible blanket of malaise over towns and cities. Vague myths of demons emerged in "normal" people's dreams in tenebrous images of incubi who lay upon sleeping women, fucking them in panting nightmares of lust and primal passions, while succubi, female demons, seduced men in their sleep, shagging them in routs of assaulting, sometime horrible pleasure that turned to exhaustion, guilt, and pain.

This disordered imaginary seemed to give to people's mad, deranged talk, their repellent, disgusting activities, their lasciviousness, their uncivilized, wild foolishness—seemed to give them a revelatory power to disclose a dimension of reality that threatened the dominion of humankind in the world. It was an imaginary that silently indwelled the heart of reasonable, moral sanity. It was an imaginary presenting the *absence* of reason that dwelled in dreams and in the reasonable faculties of reasonable people as well as indwelled the rationally defined and constructed spaces that housed embodied souls with (out) order. Order as such seemed under attack. I am not talking about irrational behavior. I am talking about sensing the absence of reason, absence of God, absence of Meaning in mortal time or in the undying universe. I am talking about the emergence of silent unreason as outcasts were set apart—divided from—and included in reason's social order.[8]

I have said that silent unreason is not a polar opposite to reason, that unreason "is" not something that contradicts reason, that there is no dichotomy between reason and unreason, and that unreason is not a thing. I imagine unreason as utter silence without Sense, Meaning, and Purpose. People can nonetheless live with mortal meanings and purposes. We can love and create, suffer, and struggle—live the whole schmear of life with no need to fill all the gaps of unreason (and unmeaning). We have our customs, our ways of governing, our ever-changing sensibilities . . . we live in mortal progressions of events, many events that can be decisive for our particular lives. Yet our lives are nomadic in the sense that there is no firm foundation for them, no fixed boundaries, no cosmic map, no ultimate purpose to define them. This sense of nomadic freedom does seem vaporous as though unreason's silent absence in the midst of rational formations and the silent absence of value and meaning in the thick of social customs and disciplines . . . as though silent absence were free-floating nothing that at times I experience as a threshold to nothing in particular . . . and thereby a threshold of possibility.

In the plotless happening of unreason—in the silent, imageless indeterminacy beyond rational boundaries, beyond the dictates of Divinities,

---

8. Unreason in Foucault's understanding emerged in the eighteenth century, in what is named the Age of Reason. The domination of reason in educated European thought at that time created not only its opposites (irrational or non-rational thought or consciousness), it also opened the way to the absence of reason . . . no reason at all. Throughout this fragment, the meaning of the word reason is vague and lacks the clarity it would seem to require of itself. As Foucault shows in *The Order of Things* (1994), rational subjectivity inevitably objectifies itself and loses the immediacy of itself that is required if it is to know itself. I am treating "reason" as a powerful imaginary formation. In the context of this book, that means that the silent limits of reason happen in the rationality that justifies reasonable authority. The suggestion is that no reason at all seems silently to shadow reasoning. A second suggestion is that rational authority and order occur as relations of power. Throughout this book I am assuming that human lives require relations of power, that "power" names a life-energy, and that people could not survive without what I identify as rational orders. That assumption in combination with the emphasis I give to imagination and images means that formations identified as rational are fragile and often need aggressive defense. Objectification and oppression are two of reason's best weapons.

beyond the grip of universalized values and the felt necessity for a stable world—a growing number of people drifted, like spirits, through silent unreason and into previously unimaginable territory. Many of them were doubtlessly odd people like Friedrich Hölderlin, J. G. Hamann, those in the Sturm und Drang movement, Charles Darwin, Friedrich Nietzsche, Mary Wollstonecraft, Rainer Maria Rilke, Søren Kierkegaard, Marquis de Sade, Jean-Jacques Rousseau, Madame de Staël, and Voltaire (to name only a few). Odd creators for their times, creative in many fields of endeavor—odd, perhaps, as they introduced new forms of intelligibility and discernment. And not-so-odd people too, like Friedrich Schleiermacher, Sigmund Freud, and Friedrich Jacobi. For all these odd and not-so-odd creative people, reason was neither a site of departure nor a goal in mind. Rather, worlds of meaning and sense began to take shape and "give to airy nothing a local habitation and name" (Shakespeare, *A Midsummer Night's Dream*). New images and conceptions that were not previously possible materialized in changing sensibilities and experiences. New anxieties also arose. Many, many new problems. With silence silencing. Like nothing nowhere. There.

Order, Rational Control, and Beyond

The lepers and then venereal-diseased people, we have seen, were declared fit for confinement. They were singled out and identified. "Normal" people knew them or knew of them as certain kinds of objects that were classified because of their disorders. Most of the abnormal ones, however, were not specifically classified. The people who babbled unintelligibly, those who had funny-shaped heads with drippy mouths hanging open, those who were hopelessly in debt, and whomever else was perceived as abnormal—all were put into houses for the exiled and confined to the spaces built with reasonable good sense. Although they were not yet bound by the rational, diagnostic nomenclature that would refine knowledge of the specific particularities of ill and disorderly people, they were nonetheless branded by reasonable people as dangerous misfits who should be confined. In short, the confined people were broadly identified and held as objects, as inmates, as rightfully condemned beings who were known by the names that condemnation bestowed on them. In the control of authorities, objectification constituted an enormous power: objects may be studied, arranged, trained, and observed. But they needn't be heard. What did they, in their *lack* of rational order, have to say worth hearing?

Rational people provided the vocabulary and order proper for defining them. These interred people were identified as not fully human, as empty of reason. In their confinement they were in the realm of reason thanks only to reasonable people's objective bestowal . . . thanks to their condemnation. These human beings themselves were outside of reason's realm when they were within it. In their perceived lack of reason, they were made unreason by their rational objectification. They silently composed silent unreason in reason's formation of them.

In this story I began with reason's ascension to social power—the growing influence of secular, rationally formed orders of good sense that were invested with unquestioned mores—with values, standards, and principles that guided people and defined what is acceptable and not acceptable in ways of living together. Individuals who chronically violated the logical orders of speaking, thinking, and evaluating, who seemed unconcerned with such orders and sense, as well as individuals who violated the communal values, transgressed the "thou shalts" and "thou shalt nots" that guided normal people—those individuals should be regulated by responsible reason. That regulation, we have seen, began in the wake of lazar houses, houses of detention that were gradually losing their inhabitants. These houses carried the memory of detaining the contagious lepers, but like a ship in a murky distance, all that was left were the traces of present-past. The good-sense detentions began to identify the detained by reference to their disease. Nothing else singled them out, individualized them. Good sense ruled. Moral rationality encircled them like an invisible barrier. As far as normal, healthy people and authoritative social leaders were concerned, those others—the barred ones—were the poxed, the mad, the socially diseased who were now reasonably housed and named. They were ordered and rationally understandable by virtue of their exile and their "gifted" identities, their objectifications.

Objectifications were combined with exclusions in such instances as people in detention houses. The purpose of detention was exclusion from communities, not healing. Inmates were connected in the community by exclusion from it. The interplay of safe social distancing and rational identification created cores of silence, silence in exilic distancing from the commonwealth, silence of objectified and muted selves, silence *in* the combinations of exclusions and objectifications, in their limits, in the inconstancy of rational order in the facilities of broken lives. The social exclusion and distancing made rational sense at that time, and the objectifications were the work of reason in re-establishing order. But the combinations of exclusion, distancing, and objective identification yielded less than an effective, governing, and reasonable structure, less than the sum of its parts. They also yielded silence *in* their combinations and interplays: exclusion, distancing, and objectification bore silence, silence *in* the removal of the exiled ones—*in* the space of their deletion, *in* their cries, their abject fear, *in* the barred wagons that carried them away; silence beyond reason and community *in* the midst of bedlam, silence *in* the raw oppression of individual lives; and silence *in* identifications that reverted to the rationality that conceived the imposed, objectifying distinctions and left people anonymous behind the names that branded them. Just silence. Inarticulable, without reason *in* the midst of unorder and the structures that contained it. Silently beyond reason's power. Unreason doing nothing. Signifying nothing.

Silence silencing in these complicities opened in and beyond the limits of reason. Opened to nowhere in particular. Beyond the good sense of the time. Beyond madness and sickness. Beyond good and evil. Beyond the objectifications. Opened, in the imagery in which I write, to unreason. Unreason: silently nowhere in particular. Without a defining image. Silence silencing and the nomadic freedom that often comes with "it."

FRAGMENT TWENTY-ONE

Spring

Veris leta facies
mundo propinatur,
hiemalis acies
victa iam fugatur,
in vestitu vario
Flora principatur,
nemorum dulcisono
que cantur celebrator.[1]

The energy of spring. Lives connecting with lives. Living connections. The soaring energy of trees as vital fluid rises from their earthen roots and moves cell by cell throughout their growing branches where leaves begin to bud and open in the silent gift of sunlight, often seeming to dance with wind, yielding themselves silently to it and restoring their movement in the world around them. Some trees bursting into color . . . Yoshino cherries, Japanese magnolias, red bud, dogwood, crabapple. . . . So many flowers. Many, many beings with new energy. I feel that vitality when I quiet my thoughts, look into a blossom, walk barefoot on warming earth. I don't have to hug a tree to feel its life. Each thing has its own energy, its own silent power. In feeling the burst of their vivacity, I forget the names, the

---

1. "Spring," *Carmina Burana*, Carl Orff. Translation: "The merry face of spring/ turns to the world,/ sharp winter/ now flees, vanquished;/ bedecked in various colors/ Flora reigns, the harmony of the woods/ praises her song/ Ah!"

categories. Their beauty is not in their reasonableness or, for me, in their orders. Their beauty is in their being silently their own.

In the reverie of spring I feel kinship with birthing and creating, be it with so little a thing as a single daffodil opening from bud to full flower. Kinship with a new song's emerging in a composer's mind. Kinship with a tree's new growth or with a new thought's beginning to open out into a changing sense of the world and the lives in it.

As I wrote these words I looked out of a window and saw a bright red cardinal on the branch of a holly tree not three feet distant, singing full-throated its mating call.

Silent intimacy with spring life might seem far removed from the processes that silently yields unreason. Unless we recall that unreason happens—happens nomadically we might say awkwardly—happens like silent birthing space . . . empty, unregulated, truant, undefined by borders, with and beyond orders. In the midst of reasonable formations, chaos—silence silencing, unreason. "Where" mutations of those formations, accompanied by stark absences of order, began to emerge as some people deviated from standards and axioms of rational clarity and good sense. "Where" in the midst of formations-cum-chaos, creations—new lives—began to be. "Where" new perspectives appeared. New world-creations arose as previous worlds of meaning and sense seemed to grow weary and lose their power that had held communities together and undesirable folks apart. Authoritative knowledge and moral suasion that had held parts of the Western world so firmly in their grip seemed to implode slowly and silently as the emptiness of unreason held open nothing to hold and rationalities seemed to reverse on themselves in an endless search for stability.

After the story of unreason's lineages, nomadic freedom, and emergence, I made this turn to spring as a reminder of birthing that also happens with silence silencing, a reminder of kinship with unreason, with new growth without reason or goodness, with beginnings that allow us to feel our kinship with the energy of lives as plants spring to new life, old hearts quicken, old flesh trembles with desire, and young cardinals sing to mate.

FRAGMENT TWENTY-TWO

The Fall of the Power of Fell Time
Abstractions Treated as Unimagined Realities

Michael Naas wrote:

"Instead of reading real life or life itself as that which precedes and gives meaning to what is called life, instead of understanding so-called life as the mere supplement to life itself, the fallen version of it, we might think of life itself as the 'invention' of what is called life, the hypostasized version of this life, an empty concept or verbal construct that has nonetheless completely transformed the Western philosophical and theological tradition. On this reading, *life itself* is the least real and the most untrue life, a mere fiction or phantasm, an illusion, in short, of what is called life. It is a reading or an interpretation that might be identified as the critique or the reversal of Platonism. . . . Instead of life itself, then, instead of the Form of life, there would be *life death* as what exceeds the neat boundaries between life and death, a life before all life forms or ideas, in short, a life before conception." Further, "life death inaugurates or opens up life at the same time as it compromises it and marks it from the start with finitude. Life death would thus name a life that is inseparable from death, a life that, through this inaugural gesture, opens time without being outside it or transcendent to it" (2018, 186, 188).

Life death in Naas's thought are words that "open up" the processes and passages of living beings. The words *life death* are not conjoined by the word *and*. He does not mean life and then death. The words name happening that is simultaneously life death. I will shift those words, life death, to *livingdying*. This shift in wording does not express disagreement. Rather, as I enter into the question of "the fall of the power of fell time" I want to draw a distinction between dying and death. *Dying* names the way lives are silently lived, the continuous passing away in lives of whatever is, the ongoing indeterminate, silent opening out of "yet to be," the strange, living "ability" of mortal beings to cease to be. Mortality is alive. *Dying* means living always in unsettling thresholds—in the present processes of ceasing to be and in the openings toward what is yet to happen. *living-dying* describes the silent eventuation of mortal lives. *Death* on the other hand, as I use the word, marks the present and permanent absence of a life once lived. *Dead* applies to a body or situation after it dies.[1] I will bring to bear the significance of this word-shift later in this riff.

Inaugurates. "Life death inaugurates or opens up life at the same time as it compromises it and marks it from the start with finitude." I interpret "inaugurates" in this context to mean that life death is an event, a site, where life death each simultaneously qualifies the other. Naas also says that life death is an "inaugural gesture" that "opens time without being outside it or transcendent to it." An important implication in that inaugural gesture is that Naas's wording immediately and silently reverts back to itself: the lively words and their interconnecting thoughts about mortality make evident their own performative event. The reversion in them performs—enacts—life death as the words speak of life death. I believe that performance means that these words intransitively compose an opening in mortal time to mortal time, that is, they compose a happening of life death. These words enact life death as they point to life death. Life death *owns*—belongs to—its finitude and discloses its mortal worldliness, its lack of otherworldly transcendence.

Does life death or time "have" agency? For reasons that will become clear, I hope, I think that neither life death nor time launches or sets in motion life death and time. They are not agents for whom transitive verbs are appropriate. Life death, rather, silently and intransitively composes a portal, a silent opening in life death to life death.

◆ ◆ ◆

A Brief Excursus on Silence

Can you feel the silence pervasive in these realities: imagining, life death, livingdying, reversions? The silence *in* the eventuations of lives? The silence

---

1. *Death* has many meanings. I note only its meaning in the context of this fragment.

pervasive of Plato's ghost in Christianity? The silence of the deep unease, the deep anxiety embodied in the power of "Life Itself?" Silence silencing of nothing in our lives gifts us with mortality.

◆ ◆ ◆

Invention. Naas's book shows the way that the image and meaning of Life Itself formed in Plato's dialogues, the way an empty concept (life) comes to have enormous power in the fiction that Life Itself is a self-standing reality of pure life—life that feigns to have severed all ties with death, undying life, LIFE ITSELF. It is an invented concept, a delusional, hypostasized formation that functions to stabilize and transcendentalize volatile, culturally generated meanings and values. The power of the image, Life Itself, silently establishes hierarchies of better and worse lives. The image gauges better and worse lives not only on the basis of the spiritual quality of various ways of living but also on the basis of intrinsically better and worse lives. Some lives are ill-fated from birth. Other lives are gifted and naturally inclined to saintly goodness as measured by their purity, sanctity, and aversion to physical desires (silent fleshly bodies: among the most corrupt and deathly aspects of living according to the lineages of Life Itself). And thickening this invented brew of power-saturated images springing from the image of Life Itself, some people can become authoritative on what Life Itself requires of all people to enable them to live blessed, earthly lives and, after passing on, to enjoy everlasting life.

The question of time is woven into the texture and power of Life Itself. If Naas's genealogy of the birth of the image, Life Itself, is correct, as I believe it is, the silent imagery that surrounds Life Itself and its silent lineages are thoroughly unaware of the hypostasizing birth of Life Itself. Thoroughly blind to its own silent mortality. Thoroughly ignorant of the emptiness that permeates it. This invented image is more destructive of lives than even uncritical rationality is when it is inclined to subject and oppress other lives. The invented, injurious image of Life Itself thrives on presenting mortal time as fell, as sinister and corrupting, as tragic and certainly not life-giving. The invention of Life Itself generated hope-instilling promises, protective power for the blessed. It generated such deeply spiritual attractions as peace of mind and prayerful communion with the Giver of Life Itself. That invention also silently generated deep, spiritual anxieties, fears, and defensive, evangelical aggressiveness as well as senses of superiority in relation to beings whose lives strayed far from harmony with shining Life Itself. This powerful delusional imagery issued forth with so many ecclesial and secular formations, ranging from beautiful works of art to guilt-engendering beliefs and values, to magical, enforced rituals. The invented image of Life Itself has silently spawned uncounted relations of power, values, meanings, rituals, and institutional formations that embody fear and hostility to livingdying, fear and hostility regarding their own lives within the provenance of fell time.

Other invented images are generated by words that are occasionally used to suggest that time itself and death itself are really alive. These hypostasizing images project agency onto time and death—the agency of time, for example, as it takes away lives or causes aging and decline. Time might heal us or flow like a river. Death might visit us as a dark, hooded figure with a long sickle hovering menacingly in the distance; death might throw a dark cloak over us or silently take our lives away. The reality of such projections are finite images; they are events of imagination that tell us what death is like, real illusions of livingdying.

We are able to think of time as nothing in particular and suffused with silence silencing if we consider timing, not as a framework for counting seconds, minutes, days, and years—not as clock time or calendar time—but rather as silent *indefinite* progressions of existences, as gathering and fading aggregations that are porous and have no apparent stable horizons. Time would then appear as silent, simultaneous, multiple sequences of random events and existences that silently emerge and silently vanish in apparently irreversible and undirected successions. "Itself" would not be an appropriate word to connect with the word, time. Time is neither an it nor an agent. And if "death" means permanent, irreversible cessation of all biological functions that sustain an organism, death (is) not a thing. Death. Utter silence.

Does silence, utter silence, motivate people to tell stories about death's origin? Motivate them to try to give it form, regardless how vague? To imagine death by drawing pictures or telling stories of death and making death an "it?" To imagine an origin for death or a cause for death's emergence, a narrated understanding of why there is death? A cause for death itself? Even the images of divine powers punishing people who have fallen out of a God's favor and have their fall to thank for the hopeless mortality of their passing lives, images of those who are cursed to live in distance from God's will, condemned to always passing pleasures and to spiritual emptiness in their disobedience, condemned to suffer everlasting agony: even such stories and images can be more bearable when they narrate—give sound and sense to—the origin and meaning of "death itself." At least, death itself is then speakable, presentable in art, objectifiable; and with some spiritual help, some people, perhaps, can overcome it. But utterly silent absence of lives? Nothing? Meaningful suffering and death as we make sense of them are much to be preferred.

Fell Time

Timber cut in one season may be called a fell. As a verb, fell can mean to cause to fall by striking, cutting, or knocking down—she felled him with one blow. It can also mean to kill—he was felled by the second shot. The meanings of fell that I have in mind when I use the word as an adjective in this fragment, however, are *lethal, meaninglessly and silently fierce*, and *capable of senseless destruction*. These meanings constitute judgments that describe mortal temporality. Mortal temporality then appears as cursed, like a spiritual disease that needs to be healed. In the context of fell time's perspective, livingdying appears as a synonym for fell time—as lethal time that is dire—dreadful. Fell time silently takes life away *in* people's living and meaninglessly brings people in their living to decline and the degeneration of old age. Fell time is permeated with deathly silence and is not a friend to stable truths. Fell time is the time of the damned, the star-crossed. It is a perceived process of taking life away in living, sometimes taking life away fiercely and always silently and senselessly. The judgment of fell time means that being mortal flesh is more like a punishment than like an opportunity.

❖ ❖ ❖

A Brief Excursus: Flesh

Fell mortal time is often associated with flesh in Christian faith. A few examples: "For to set the mind on the flesh is death, but to set the mind on the Spirit is life and peace" (Romans 8:6). "For if you live according to the flesh you will die, but if by the Spirit you put to death the deeds of the body, you will live" (Romans 8:13). "For I say, walk by the Spirit, and you will not gratify the desires of the flesh" (Galatians 5:16). "And those who belong to Christ Jesus have crucified the flesh with its passions and desires" (Galatians 5:24).

♦ ♦ ♦

But what happens if the image of fell time falls from its force, from its judgmental power in our everyday lives. What happens if people affirm their lives as livingdying? If people find meanings that give them purpose, joy if they are fortunate, motivation to live as well as they can in their acceptance of their mortality? If the processes of livingdying are experienced as ordinary and affirmable and people find ways to carry out their fleshly lives with care, meaning, and, when possible, pleasure?

Fell time, complementary to Life Itself as Naas finds it, is an invention, a powerful formation of a group of images that encage livingdying in narratives, values, and beliefs that condemn the ways mortal lives happen. Affirmative meanings for livingdying, on the other hand, can "open up life at the same time it compromises [living] with finitude." Fell time too is an "empty concept," an "hypostasized version" of time that turns lives away from themselves.[2] It silently inaugurates occlusions of lives' own awe-inspiring physical vitality and constitutes a confusion of imaginary reality with living events. Fell time's fall from social and religious power can free people from those occlusions, clear people's imaginations of fell time's silent, destructive distortions.

In the opening that is gifted by fell time's fall from power, will people accept time's timing as nothing in particular? Are we able to affirm time as no thing, as irreversible and undirected progressions of multiple sequences of events that silently emerge and silently transform or vanish? If circumstances allow, can we feel in our progressions astonishment with our living as we own our dying? Can we own our livingdying *in* our livingdying without feeling ourselves transcendent to it? If we are fortunate, are we able to intensify our mortal lives with meanings that generate hope and desire more life? Live amazed—in wonder—in our mortality, in our flesh, in our ability to be, to create, to love and be loved?

---

2. I am using Naas's words from the first paragraph of this fragment in the quoted words and phrases.

FRAGMENT TWENTY-THREE

A Story about Two Lovers in Pervading Silence Silencing

In the Beginning

A tall, slender, young woman with long, dark hair whom I did not know was standing at my back door in Nashville, Tennessee. A young man stood next to her. He had written his dissertation with me at Vanderbilt University, we were friends, and he wanted me to meet his partner. It was raining, the back door was close to the end of the driveway, her partner knew the house well from departmental picnics and dinners and didn't need to go around to the front door. I welcomed them, and we talked for a while. I assume we talked. I do not remember what we talked about. That was 1980. I did not remember her name until I received an invitation from her.

Prelude to Friendship

The invitation was to give a lecture at Southern Illinois University (SIU) where she, Nancy Tuana, was an assistant professor of philosophy. She and her partner also invited me to stay at their home. I felt welcomed and comfortable in their hospitality.

    She was indeed tall and slender. Her lovely, wavy dark hair flowed down her back, at least a foot or two long, I thought. She was a striking person—a bit reserved but an individual with strength and independence that I could feel along with another quality I could not quite identify.

When she looked at me as we talked, she opened a space of neutral friendliness and welcome. She had a quality of lightness and brightness, one of good energy—often characteristic of people who care about what is happening in the world. Not intimidating. Wide open eyes, attentive, very present . . . very *there*. Quite beautiful. She and he seemed much in love. I recall particularly sitting in the kitchen while she prepared breakfast, when he reached up to pat her hips as she stood on a stool and stretched to reach something on the top shelf. The atmosphere was warm and pleasant in the feelings of friendship with him and with her hospitality and easy laughter. She came from a very different philosophical background than mine and had little to say after I presented a lecture on Martin Heidegger.

Time passed. Memories faded.

I came to know of Nancy Tuana as a distant colleague, but for over a decade I had no occasions where our paths crossed after my visit at SIU.

Our paths did cross in the mid-1990s in Eugene at the University of Oregon. She was one of the two primary leaders in the philosophy department. Three of the young faculty members in the department were former students of mine, and over a period of time I had occasions to give two invited lectures as well as attend two conferences there. Nancy and I talked now and then on those occasions and had several meals together. I admired her and began looking forward to seeing her when I went to Eugene. That quality I could not quite identify at Southern Illinois University came out clearly as I came to know her better. It was her natural leadership ability and administrative skills combined with her frequent smile and laughter that put people at ease and drew them to her. Quite remarkable.

One of my lasting memories from the Oregon visits is Nancy's opening a door while I was giving a lecture, opening it just enough to check the audience, catch my eye, and smile. Then closing the door quietly.

A Silence Begins

Nancy joined the faculty at Penn State University in 2001 as the Dupont/Class of 1949 Professor of Philosophy and the founding director of the Rock Ethics Institute. The Institute was a big deal with a large endowment gift to develop programs that would have impact in many departments and colleges throughout the university. I had joined the faculty there six years earlier. She asked me to be a member of her advisory board.

Working with Nancy was a pleasure. We both had a considerable amount of administrative experience and were attuned to each other in ways that made cooperation and (in my case) learning how to set up and run an ethics institute a pleasure. I felt an openness between us, a reciprocal flow of understanding and good will. The Institute thrived in her leadership. There was also another factor that emerged during the years we worked together: we began to feel attracted to each other physically as well as personally. And the attraction grew. We were both married and monogamous and never mentioned those feelings of attraction to each other. We each knew that it was dangerous territory, that we could destroy our friendship. No touching. At all. It was a silent, erotic draw. Very silent. We were nonetheless happy when we were together; and when needed, we had each other's back. Then, due to departmental politics, things got really rough, and we learned that we could trust each other completely. By the time a new philosophy department chair was installed the department's cohesion was torn apart, and its graduate program was temporarily closed. I was offered and accepted a position at Vanderbilt University to develop a new University Center for Ethics and to take a university chair. The departure was sad, but I took with me the depth of Nancy's and my friendship, attraction, and trust that we each had for the other.

Interlude

Our friendship survived the geographical distance between us. Nancy and I talked by phone every two months or so, catching up, gossiping, chit-chatting. In 2006 I invited her to come to Vanderbilt and lead a workshop on engineering ethics. In 2010 I had serious arrhythmia and received a pacemaker. A week after the pacemaker was in place, I flew to Italy and a philosophy institute where I was slated to give a week-long course. It was a considerable challenge since I was still recovering from the effects of the arrhythmia and the procedure. To my surprise, Nancy came to Italy (in support of me, I believe) in spite of her demanding work at Penn State. During that week we had long conversations on walks by a small river close to the hotel that housed the institute. My feelings for her intensified. In 2011 Nancy planned and hosted a three-day symposium on my philosophical work with a dozen philosophers from across the country. By the end of the week, regardless the silence between us, I thought she loved me. I knew that I loved her.

In December of 2012 and after a long struggle I gave up on my marriage. All the paperwork was done by March 2013 for the amicable divorce. In mid-May I realized that with all the distractions I had not spoken with Nancy for several months. When I called her, I learned that she too had been heavily occupied with family issues and that she was one signature away from being divorced.

Breaking the Silence

At the end of that long conversation about Nancy's extremely difficult previous two years, she said, "I have been living alone for a year, and I believe I have worked through the emotions I needed to address. Some of my friends are encouraging me to begin dating. I'm not about to sign up for a dating service, as some of them are suggesting, but I am considering the possibility of dating." Before saying good-bye, I said that I would call her in a few weeks to check in and see how she's doing. After I clicked off, I stared out the window. I had had no idea that she would be available. I wanted to be with her. And *I* am available! Maybe I had a chance. Instead of waiting a few weeks, I called two days later. I remember beginning by saying, "let me tell you what's been going on in my life." I gave her the full story. She said, "I didn't know all of that," referring primarily to my divorce. Then she said, "I have been living alone for a year, and I believe I have worked through the emotions I needed to address. Some of my friends are encouraging me to begin dating . . ." I interrupted, "I want to be on your list." At that moment, Nancy fell totally silent.

As the seconds began to pass, I looked nervously at my watch and started counting them as I thought, "Shit. I might have just killed a wonderful friendship." She told me later that while we were talking, she was sitting on the ground in a corner of her fenced back yard and pulling weeds. When I said I wanted to be on her list, she thought, "What did he say!? . . . Shit . . . If I misunderstood him, I could ruin our wonderful friendship."

She was silent, sitting, not moving, in that shaded corner. For over a minute and a half, she was silent! Utterly silent. I was in despair, holding the phone in one hand, my head on the palm of my other hand, leaning down, thinking, "Oh my God, what have I done? *What have I done*?!" Finally, Nancy said softly and matter-of-factly, "Would you repeat that, please?" In a voice considerably less robust than when I first said what I wanted, I repeated, "I would like to be on your list." And with the following words, the years-long stretch of that silence between us was broken, overridden by the words: "I would welcome you on my list."

Free at Last

The gates of attraction, long closed, were opened. We had never hugged, never kissed. But now our feelings poured out, released, joyful, sensual, sexy. We wanted to know everything about each other, reaching out to the other in the silence of distance with simple, deep pleasure in hearing the other's voice, in the emailed words, in the bonding that grew firm and deepened. Surprised by the joy that neither of us had expected to find in the remainder of our lives.

Both of us were occupied with obligations until July, Nancy in State College, I in Nashville. But we emailed throughout the days and talked (and talked and talked) at night until the edge of sleep allowed only a murmured, "Good night. Sleep well, my love." After a few weeks, we didn't just love each other. We had fallen completely *in* love with each other. Our first kiss, in case you're interested, was on July 5, 2013, in the State College airport. I was about to turn seventy-eight. Nancy was about to turn sixty-two.

As we exited the airport, a friend of Nancy's looked at us and said, "You're lit up like a Christmas tree!"

We continue to be very much in love.

Silence pervades this love. It—this love—is utterly silent feeling. No set of symbols captures such feeling. No reason justifies the love. No words suffice. It's a little bit like Nancy's opening a door just enough to catch my eye and smile. But the door doesn't close. It opens wide into a silent space where we are silently, so silently joined. I too smile, a deep smile, a deep, silent, joyful smile. We are always in our love's threshold, a threshold that needs loving nurture as it opens in silence and onto the next moments with the possibilities of joy, trust, play, companionship, conflict, anger, sickness, grief, pain, and sorrow. Even when I am distracted, upset, or concentrating as I, writing these words, am now, I feel the open door. I feel her smile. I feel my love of her joining her love of me, both at once, as if one.

All of this in silence, beyond the words and murmured sounds begotten of love. In pervading, unrestrained silence silencing, loves, like an emerging sunrise or a flash of lightening or a full moon in a quiet night—loves too, really, vastly exceed all images that arise from them. As though in airy nothing, loves body forth in feelings, in the five hundred thousand actions and words that are born of them. Body forth in measureless silence in which loves live and in which loves will die.

◆ ◆ ◆

Epilogue. Until I and This Love Are No More

A friend of mine who read a draft of my text suggested that I change the last words, "will die," to "may die." That would be a major change. My decision is not to change the wording and its meaning. I believe that I understand why he would prefer "may." Here is my response. I address him directly in what follows with the familiar "you."

You suggest, in the context of "measureless silence," the phrasing "loves may die," instead of "loves will die." The word "may," as I believe you intend it, suggests that love might be eternal, might be forever, might be divine and have a stretch beyond anything we can know.

There is indeed silence, you say. But for me, measureless silence—silence silencing—is not framed by the silence you mention, the silence of not knowing. Silence silencing (is) silence of nothing. Silence silencing, not a state of uncertainty, not an issue of undecidability. Loves as I am speaking of them are feelings that have no other existence than their happening in individuals (with all their mystery and magic). For me there is no "maybe" there. "Maybe" suggests knowledge and its limits. I repeat, loves are feelings, not knowledge. It's all about bodying. Loves engender certain kinds of knowledge. But knowledge *about* loves comes later, doesn't it? Comes in relation to loves' occurrences and does the best it can under the circumstances? Isn't "ever" only *now,* long before imagination and knowledge have a go with it? Don't you like the image of knowledge in its wisdom, perhaps in its fear or in its longing having a go with a love? Aren't loves beyond knowledge? Far beyond?

I can imagine many reasons and motives for imagining love as possibly enduring in an indeterminate ever—*ever*, not conceived in the *imagery* of a timeline but *imagined* as wonderfully *now* without end. But I cannot convincingly envisage *images* as having a life beyond the mortal repetitions and feelings that sustain them. I am thinking of silence silencing exceeding imaginative formations and feelings. Like death exceeding all imagery. The mortality of loves and images of love compose something we best accept. Doesn't that make loves all the more beautiful and demanding? Frightening, perhaps, in their vulnerability? Yet, all the more wonderful because of their vulnerability? Loves living and dying in silence? To be in love, feeling its transforming passage in my life, feeling love's sense of *ever* in its passing moments, and wanting to live, to LIVE in it until I and this love are no more?

References

Cummings, E. E. 1991. *E. E. Cummings Complete Poems 1904–1962*. Edited by George J. Firmage. New York: Liveright Publishing Corporation and London: W. W. Norton & Co. Ltd.

Dylan, Bob. 1965. Interview with Nora Ephron & Susan Edmiston. https://www.interferenza.net/bcs/interw/65-aug.htm.

Foucault, Michel. 1973. *Madness and Civilization: A History of Madness in the Age of Reason*. Translated by Richard Howard. New York: Vintage Books.

Foucault, Michel. 1994. *The Order of Things: An Archaeology of the Human Sciences*. New York: Vantage Books.

Foucault, Michel. 2001. *Power: The Essential Works of Foucault, 1954–1984, Volume 3*. Edited by James D. Faubion, translated by Robert Hurley. New York: New Press.

Foucault, Michel. 2006. *The History of Madness*. Edited by Jean Khalfa, translated by Jonathan Murphy and Jean Khalfa. London and New York: Routledge.

Jeffers, Robinson. 2001. *The Selected Poetry of Robinson Jeffers*. Edited by Tim Hunt. Stanford: Stanford University Press.

Kierkegaard, Søren. 1987. *Either/Or*. Translated by Edna H. Hong and Howard V. Hong. Princeton: Princeton University Press.

Krell, David Farrell. 1990. *On Memory, Remembrance, and Writing: On the Verge*. Bloomington: Indiana University Press.

Kren, Thomas, Diane Waldman, and Nancy Spector. 1997. *Art of this Century: The Guggenheim Collections*. New York: The Solomon R. Guggenheim Foundation.

Lawrence, D. H. 1928. *Lady Chatterley's Lover*. New York: Grove Press Inc.

Lowery, David. 2017. *A Ghost Story*. United States: A24.

Naas, Michael. 2018. *Plato and the Invention of Life*. New York: Fordham University Press.

Nietzsche, Friedrich. 1966. *Beyond Good and Evil*. Translated by Walter Kaufmann. New York: Random House.

Nietzsche, Friedrich. 1997. *Daybreak: Thoughts on the Prejudices of Morality.* Edited by Maudemarie Clark and Brian Leiter, translated by R. J. Hollingdale. Cambridge: Cambridge University Press.

Oliver, Mary. 2004. *Why I Wake Early.* Boston, Massachusetts: Beacon Press.

Orff, Carl. 1968. *Carmina Burana.* Hamburg: Deutsche Grammophon.

Richard, Nelly. 2004. *The Insubordination of Signs: Political Change, Cultural Transformation, and Poetics of the Crisis.* Translated by Alice A. Nelson and Silvia R. Tanderciaz. Durham, NC: Duke University Press.

Rivera, Omar. 2020. "Cataclysms: Elemental Exposures of the Cosmic Past" (unpublished manuscript).

Rivera, Omar. 2021. *Andean Aesthetics and Anticolonial Resistance.* Bloomsbury, England: Bloomsbury Publications.

Scott, Charles. 1999. *The Time of Memory.* Albany: State University of New York Press.

Scott, Charles. "Virginia's House" (unpublished poem).

Shakespeare, William. *A Midsummer Night's Dream.* Edited by Barbara A. Mowat and Paul Werstine. Folger Shakespeare Library.

Shakespeare, William. *The Tempest.* Edited by Barbara A. Mowat and Paul Werstine. Folger Shakespeare Library.

Stevens, Wallace. 1971. "Mere Being." In *The Palm at the End of the Mind,* edited by Holly Stevens. New York: Vintage Books.

Tuana, Nancy, and Charles Scott. 2020. *Beyond Philosophy: Nietzsche, Foucault, Anzaldúa.* Bloomington: Indiana University Press.

Turner, Elizabeth Hutton. 1999. *Georgia O'Keeffe: The Poetry of Things.* New Haven: Yale University Press.

Valleja, Alejandro. "Silencio Vivencial/Germinal Silences" (unpublished manuscript).

Index

absence, 41, 54–55; of anything, 67; death and, 92–93; feel of, 63–64; in living presence, 83–84; longing and, 86–87; of predefined definitive world-order, 57–58; with present things and lives, 18; of reason, 111–12; silent, 70–71, 78, 100, 110; in space, 84; undefined, 70–71
abyss, 83–84
affects, affective, 3–4; attunement with silence silencing, 8, 12; awareness, 48–49; bondages and boundaries of, 1–2; disclosing, 2; everyday, 1–2; feelings and, 4, 4n5; as immediate, non-reflective, 2, 93; as new enlivening, 12; of now, 51; revealing, 11; touch and, 93; understanding and, 17–18. *See also* feeling; poietic creation
agency, 4, 71–72, 119, 121
airy nothing, 85–88, 112–13, 128–29
Alive Hospice (Nashville, TN), 5–6
ambiguity, 18, 32–33, 35–36, 76
ambivalence, 33–34
Anne, 88–91, 94. *See also* touch, touching
anomaly, anomalous, 7n7, 8–9, 31–32, 44, 76–77
anxiety, 4, 24–25, 29, 65, 75, 80, 84–85, 109–10, 119–20

Aphrodite, 34–35
Apollo, 32–33
architecture, 3, 50–53
Ares, 34–35
argument, argumentation, 3, 61, 65
Aristotle, 33
art of living, 24–25
astonishment, 29–30, 41–42, 52–53, 67–68, 75, 84–86, 123
Athena, 35–36
attempters, 58–59, 67. *See also* Nietzsche, Friedrich; riddles, riddlers
attunement: beyond conception, 7–8; with fluid and unpredictable transformations, 35–36; to holding completions in abeyance, 64–65; with riddle of being alive, 60–61; with silence silencing, 1–2, 4–5, 7–8, 12, 24, 39–40, 44; in touch, 89; to unreason, 76–79
awareness: without bifurcation or justification, 19; of creative experiences, 53; *in* difference, 7–8, 38–39; of dying, 5–6; feeling and, 38–39, 48–49; held by nuance, intimation, and implication of interactive words, 48–49; of home's *Unheimlichkeit*, 98–99; immediacy of, 2, 2n1, 4, 39, 91–93; lineages

133

awareness *(continued)*
  of, 66–67; non-reflective, 39; of nothing, 83–84; ordinary, 23; poet's, 85–86; reflective, 91–92; of and in shifting ambiguities, 35–36; *in* silence silencing, 1–2, 2n3, 3, 12, 14, 36–39, 43–44, 53, 81–82, 100; as tantalizing, 9–10; of touching, 92–94; undifferentiated, 41; of what we cannot say directly, 34
awe, 4–5, 123

beauty, 4, 20–21, 29–30, 54, 100, 116–17; empty and indifferent, 54–55
becoming, 65, 87
Beethoven, Ludwig van, *Ninth Symphony*, 24–25
between-being, 18–19
bifurcations, 19, 41, 61, 67–68, 71–72, 74–78, 105
bird song, 9–10, 12–14, 43
birth, birthing, 4, 19, 29–30, 32–33, 52–53; creative experience as, 50, 57–58, 62, 73–74, 117; to dancing stars, 64; of images, 85–86, 120–21; of new prospects, 65; touch and, 89
Black Mesa, 53–54
blindness, 29–30, 60, 91, 120–21; blinded by light, 45–47, 101
body: bodysoul, 86–87; bodythoughts, 65; embodied life, 64–65; as flesh, 122–23; gap in, 19; life and, 120; memory and, 18; mindbody, 83–84; permeated by silence, 1–2; racialized, 90; skin, 89–91, 94. *See also* touch, touching
borders, 7–8, 19, 32; border art, 35; as porous, 58–59; silence and, 35, 44, 58–59, 83; unreason and, 117
boundaries, 1, 10; as dynamic, porous, and fluid, 3–4, 32–33; of poietic activities, 3–4; silence and, 8, 80; without, 8, 81–82, 85–86, 112–13, 118
breaches, breaching, 67–68, 70–71, 105, 110–11; unreason and, 72–79
breeze, 9–10, 13–14, 37, 49, 102

car crash, 82
Carmina Burana (Carl Orff), 116–17
caves, 4–5
cavities, 85–88
cellars, 8
chaos, 9, 49–50, 57–58, 64–65, 117; free spiritedness and, 58–59, 65; happening of, 67; silent, 49, 64–65, 67, 75; wonder and, 86. *See also* order; unreason
Chile, military coup of 1973, 17–18, 18n2
city grid, 3
closeness, 13–14, 88–89, 88n2, 97–98. *See also* touch, touching
Colapietro, Vincent, 11n1
communication, 11–12, 31–34, 44, 48, 48–49, 101, 111
communion with Divinity, 5, 120–21
community, 18–19, 34–35, 117; exclusion from, 73, 114–15; leprosy and, 69n7, 71, 73, 77, 109–10, 114–15
conceive, conceptualize, 2–4, 6–8, 80; beyond, 18, 33, 38–39, 48, 55n4, 57, 81–83, 91, 94; creation and, 62–64, 86; empty concept, 118, 120, 123; unreason and, 69n6, 106–11, 113–15
confinement, 73–74, 105–6, 113–14
conformity, 15
connection, disconnection, 18–19, 38, 70–72, 77–78, 82–83, 92–93, 99, 100, 103, 114–17, 119
Connie, 15–16

contagion, 34, 77–78, 109–11. *See also* leprosy; unreason
contemplation, 84–85
conversation, 9, 11, 35, 66, 93–95
corpse, 79–80, 92–93. *See also* death, dying
creativity, 3–5, 19; as birthing, 50, 57–58, 62, 73–74, 117; experience of, 51–52, 57–58, 62–65, 68–69; silent, 50; space of, 85–87; unreason and, 112–13. *See also* poietic creation
cummings, e e, 39–40, 48–49; "Beautiful," 20–21
custom, 22, 32–33, 112

dancing, 94–95
dancing star, 57–58, 64, 86. *See also* Nietzsche, Friedrich
darkness, 26–28, 37, 39, 46n1, 71–72, 74, 100–103, 109–10; of desert, 53–54; light and, 17n1, 34, 40, 45–47, 84, 95; silence and, 89
Darwin, Charles, 112–13
de Staël, Madame, 112–13
death, dying, 66–67, 87, 118–19, 119n1; agency of, 121; awareness of, 5–6, 15; creativity and, 62–63; deeper, 40; experience of, 41–42; imminence of, 29; life and, 98, 118–23, 129–30; as not-it, 41; silence and, 41–42, 92–93, 121–22; touching, 92–3. *See also* life, living
deformation, 10, 32, 98
dementia, 26–29
depression, 84
desert, 16, 53–56, 81–82
deserted together, 53–56
desire, 4–5, 86–88, 89n2, 103, 106–7, 117, 120, 122–23; blind, 59–60
detachment, 29–30
devotion, devoted love, 87

dialectics, 18
diaphanous, 2, 23–24, 85–86
Diderot, Denis, 75n9
difference, 3–4, 12, 21, 24, 55, 110; awareness *in*, 38–39; between, 70–71; breaching, 71–73, 76–79; degrees of, 59–61; touching, 94–96
dignity, 15–16, 103
Dilthey, Wilhelm, 34–35
disaster, 100
discipline, 1, 59n3, 77–78, 112. *See also* knowledge; objectification, objectivity
disclosure, 2–3, 11–12, 48, 54–55, 58–59, 66–68, 74, 87, 111–12, 119
discord, 5, 52–53
discovery, 12, 45–47, 50, 60, 62
disease, 69–70, 73, 77–78, 106–10, 113–14, 122
dismemberment, 17–19
disorientation, 5, 17–18
disposability, 29
dispossession, 26–28
distance, 15, 60–61, 88–89, 98, 121–22; social distancing, 114–15
distractions, 1, 5, 104, 111
divisions, 67–71, 70n8, 77–78; breaching, 73–74, 76, 78–79; inclusion and, 110; silent, 71
dreams, dreaming, 12, 29–30, 40, 71–72, 76–77, 86–87, 109–12; dreaming innocence, 89–91, 89n2
dwell, dwelling, 22–23, 111–12; no dwelling, non-dwelling, 49, 77–78; with silence, 26–28; *unheimlich* space and, 84–85
Dylan, Bob, 48–50, 49n1; continuous movement in silence of music-not-yet, 50; experience of writing and performing music, 57–58

ek-stasis, 12, 50, 85–86

136 | Index

empathy, 34
empty, emptiness, 17–18, 17n1, 53–56, 81–86, 81n1, 108, 113–14; empty concept, 118, 120, 123; empty room, 9. *See also* vastness
encompassing, 38
enjoyment, 24–25, 59–61, 94–95, 120
environment, 1–2, 5, 84, 95, 105–6
epilogue, 29–30, 129–30
Escena de Avanzada art movement, 18n2
essential thing, 68–69
estrangement, 5
evasiveness, 35–36
events, 13–14, 43–44, 46–47, 53, 64, 68–69, 112, 118–19, 121, 123; imagined, 23–24, 100, 121; particularity of, 34; poietic, 4, 62, 65; silence and, 5, 8, 57, 78; telling, 11–12; of touching, 92
everyday: affective bondages and boundaries of, 1–2; awareness of dying, 5–6; dust of, 51–53; ever-present potential happening of violence, 17–18; experience, 11–12, 23, 93; going beyond, 51; indirect and performative dimensions of communicating, 11–12
exclusion, 69–71, 77–78, 108, 110, 114–15
exile, exilic, 18–19, 70–71, 73–74, 77–79, 106–8, 110–11, 113–15; exilic confinement, 73–74, 105–6, 108–15; exilic freedom, 69–71, 69n7, 77–78. *See also* between-being; nomads, nomadic
experience: of awe in flow of lives, 4–5; being alive in insubstantiality of, 2; creative, 50–51, 53, 57–58, 62–65, 68–69; of darkness, 45–46; of death, 41–42; everyday, 11–12, 23, 93; of inattentiveness, 93; of indefiniteness, 66–67; of inexpressible, 48–49; of loss and trauma, 82–84; of movement, 51; new ways of, 68–69; non-creative, 51–52; non-objective, 50–51; sensing, 101–2; of silence, 46–47, 53, 55–56, 100; of what might yet be possible, 49, 57–58
experiment, experimentation, 50, 61–62, 65
explain, explanation, 6–7, 14, 31–32, 55, 64

falling unmeaning, 20–21
fear, 4, 40, 71–72, 80, 114–15, 120–21, 129
feelings, 4–5; of absence, 83, 86–87; of awareness, 38–39, 91–92; beyond, 10; of change, 63–64; of closeness, 89n2; come first, 38–40; as embodied, 65; happening of, 16; imaginative, 11–12; immediacy of, 13–14, 91–93; of indeterminate presence, 23–24; knowledge and, 38–39, 129; of love, 87; mutual, 91; of nothing, 29, 86; of now, 51; reflection and, 13–14, 91–92; *in* silence silencing, 23, 37–40, 44, 57, 86, 97–98, 119–20; space of, 23; toward specific ways of relating, 19; touch and, 89–91, 94, 96; understanding and, 17–18; as undifferentiated background *in* awareness, 38–39; unreason and, 75; untruth of unmeaning silence, 21. *See also* affects
fell time, 118–23
Fichte, Friedrich Gottlieb, 75n9
forests, 15–16, 103–4
forgetting, 24–25, 54–55, 116–17
form, formation, 3–5, 7–8, 10, 31–32, 66–67, 74, 94–95; beyond, 54, 76,

81, 84–87; breaking in speechless disclosure, 11–12; formless, 9, 98; imaginative, 3–4, 57–58, 60–62, 98, 100, 106–7, 123, 129–30; of life, 118, 120–21, 123; of reason, 36, 76–77, 106–9, 110, 112–14, 112n8, 117; silence and, 9, 44, 66–68, 78–81, 98, 113–14; unform, 4–5, 74–75, 78–79. *See also* deformation

Foucault, Michel, 66–69, 69n9, 74, 76, 106n2; *The History of Madness*, 67–68, 68n5, 71; on unreason, 69–70, 77–78, 110, 112n8

fracture, 18, 20–21, 33

fragility, 2, 101–2, 112n8

fragments, 3, 3n4, 109–10

free spirits, free spiritedness, 58–62, 64–65, 67, 78–79

freedom, 26–27, 49–50, 59–60, 69–71, 74–75, 77–78, 95, 105–10, 112, 115, 117. *See also under* exile, exilic; nomads, nomadic

Freeman, Cornelia and Paul, 94–96

Freud, Sigmund, 112–13

Gadamer, Georg, 34–35

gap, 18–19, 72–73, 78–79; in body, 19; as indeterminate opening, 19; silent, 35, 82–84

garden, 3, 8, 97–98

gender, 43; pronouns, 33–34

ghosts, 22–24, 54, 86

Ghost Story, A (dir. David Lowery), 24–25, 24n1

grasswind, 23

Guggenheim Museum (New York City), 50–53, 50n3; Reading Room, 51–52; spiraling ramp, 51

Guggenheim, Solomon R., 50n3

gun shot, 43–44

Hamann, J. G., 112–13

happening: of chaos, 67; of discovery, 47; feeling, 16; of life death, 188–19; of love, 87; nomadic, 117; nothing, 78–80; performative, 11–12; presence and, 14, 17–18; of silence, 38, 53–54, 66, 78–79, 81–82, 87; of touch, 90, 93–94; of unreason, 112–13, 117

haunt, haunting, 22–25; absence and, 86–87; presence and, 49, 54–55; of unreason, 72–73, 110

hearing, 12, 23

Hegel, G. W. F., 64

Heidegger, Martin, 34–35, 76n10

Helios, 46n1

Hephaestus, 34–35

hermeneutics, 7n7, 32–33, 32n2; as art of interpreting, 6–7; lineages of, 35. *See also* Hermes; interpretation

Hermes, 7n7, 32–35, 44; hermeneutics and, 32–33, 35; Hermes Trismegistus (thrice Great God), 33, 35; power of restless, unresolved instability and unclarity, 33–35; as trickster, 34–35

Hippolyta. *See* Shakespeare, William, *A Midsummer Night's Dream*

Hölderlin, Friedrich, 112–13

home: haunting, 23–24; homelessness, 18, 23; silence and, 23, 26–29; *uheimlich*, 98–99

Homer, 34–35

horror, 24–25

Hume, David, 75n9

identity, identification: as between-being, 18–19; feeling differently, 63–64; going beyond, 103–4; indeterminate, 59; lack of, 8–9, 32; mixed, mingled, and blurred boundaries of, 33; presence and,

identity, identification *(continued)*
4–5; temptation of, 67; uncertainty and, 83
images, 3, 9–10, 13–14, 24–25, 87, 128–30; creativity and, 63–64, 85–86, 112–13; of forced-truths, 60; immediacy of, 63–64; of life, 120–23; memory and, 47, 92–93; reason and, 74, 76–77, 79, 106–13, 112n8, 115; senses and, 101–2; silence and, 5–6, 38, 67–68, 78–79, 81–82, 98–100, 115
imaginaries, 67–68, 68n4, 106–7; airy nothing and, 86; unreason and 69–79, 109–12
imagination, 3–4, 11, 11n1; beyond, 40; creative power of, 85–86; experience of, 50–51, 54–55; indirection and, 10; instability of, 105–7; metaphor and, 48–49; nomadic space of, 107; opening to what is left out, 57; products of, 24–25; reality of, 23–24; silent, 48–49, 98–101; space of, 85–86. *See also* creativity
immanence, 8, 95
immateriality, 23–24
immediacy, 2, 91–92; affective disclosing and, 2–3; awareness and, 2n1, 4, 38–39; in experiences of creativity, 63; inspirited, 52–53, 62; of sense, 11–14, 93; of silence, 41, 62; of touch, 89–95
in-between, 14, 26–28, 94–95
in-spiriting, 12, 52–53, 62
inaugurate, 118–19, 123
incubi, 111
indefiniteness, 32, 44, 49, 57–61, 71–72; experience of, 66–67; silent, 60–61, 67, 75, 121
indeterminacy, 23–24, 32–34; of future, 95; of silence, 39, 67; thresholds of, 67–68, 76, 95; unreason and, 75–79; of yet-to-be, 67–68
indifference, 13–14, 53–56, 75, 107
indirections, 3, 6–7, 10–12, 31–32, 35–36, 38, 44, 62
industrialization, 15
inexhaustible treasure, 29–30
innocence, 45–46, 90; dreaming, 89n1, 91
insensitivity, 1–2
insentience, 15
instability, 35–36, 58–59, 105–7
intensity, 12, 15, 34, 48–49, 61–62, 84–85, 87, 104
interpretation: indeterminacy of, 33–34, 36; by indirection, 6–7, 33, 44; lived, 64; of silence, 6–7, 31–32, 44. *See also* hermeneutics; knowledge
intimacy, 89–90, 94–95, 117
intuition, 3–4, 48
invention, 80, 118, 120–21, 123
invisibility, 18–19, 31–32, 44, 98, 111, 114
inwardness, 15–16, 103
irony, 60–61
irrealis mood, 7–8, 8n8, 37n1
itinerate, 32–33. *See also* nomads, nomadic

jackhammers, 51–53
Jacobi, Friedrich, 112–13
James, William, 75n9
Jeffers, Robinson, "The Treasure," 29–30
joy, 10, 29–30, 40, 84, 87, 97, 106–7, 123, 128
judgment, 14, 34, 68n4, 69–71, 76, 106–7, 122–23; without, 63–65, 87, 94–96, 99

Kahlo, Frida, 75n9

Key Theater, 88–90
Kierkegaard, Søren, 75n9, 76n10, 112–13; *Either/Or*, 89n2
kingdom of truth, 108–9
kinship, 15, 54–55, 103–4, 108–11, 117
kiss, 13–14, 40, 95, 128
kitchen, 4–5, 49–50, 84, 124–25
knowledge: authoritative, 117; bifurcating divisions of, 67–68, 71–72; breaching, 76; as changeable, 61; feeling and, 38–39, 129; ignorance and, 59–60; morality and, 36; secular order of, 73–75; unreason and, 75
Krell, David Farrell, 81n2

language: beyond literal expression, 20–21, 29–30, 35–36, 40, 48–49, 55; developing, 8; indirect and performative dimensions of, 11–12; interpretation and, 31–34, 44; logics of, 20–21, 35–36, 59–61, 66; nomadic, 33; poietic, 4, 9–10; of silence, 36
laughter, 61, 63–65
laws (nómos), 32–33
lazar houses, 77–78, 105–6, 108, 114
leprosy , 69n7, 69–74, 77–78, 106–8, 110, 113–14. *See also* unreason
life, living: affirmation of, 34; art of, 24–25; in awareness, 38–39, 44; beyond, 29–30, 51; covering over threat of silence silencing's breaching, 79–80; death and, 5–6, 98, 118–23, 129–30; without definitive answers, 44; embodied, 64; everyday, 11–12, 51; as exploration into unknown territory, 65; flow of, 4–5; gaiety of, 61–62; hierarchies of better and worse, 120–21; indefinite incompleteness of, 57–61; indifference and, 53–56; life-gap, 18–19; life-revealing, 34–35; life-spaces, 84–85, 87; liveliness, 15–16; memory and, 24, 26–28; new enlivening, 12; as nomadic, 112; with others, 24–25; other-than-human, 2; with past, 19; without sense of measured time, 13–14; as shifting, passing, often unpredictable, 4–5; silence and, 8–9, 12, 38–39, 44, 53–55, 79–80, 103–4; uncertainty and, 83; unidentifiable, 58–60; unreason and, 67–68; vitality and, 116–17; ways of, 58–59, 87. *See also* death, dying
life death, livingdying, 118–23
life itself, 118–23
light, 23, 31–33, 31n1, 39, 40, 41, 52–54, 82, 99–103, 116–17; darkness and, 17n1, 34, 40, 45–47, 46n1, 84, 95; reason and, 74, 107; of salvation, 73; silence of, 46–47, 84
lightness, 34–35, 44, 124–25
lightning, 101–2, 128–29
lineages, 46–47, 117, 120–21; of expulsion, 105–8; fragmented, 110; forming, 80; gap in, 35; institutional, 60–61; lawlessness of, 33–34; as lively, 74; sensibilities and, 66–67, 69n6, 73–74; unification and, 5
longing, 86–87, 129
loss, 15–16, 26–28, 34, 40, 63, 84, 101
love, 26–29, 86–87; devotion and, 87; knowledge and, 129; "loves will die," 128–30; silence and, 128–30; time of, 129–30
lovebeyondwords, 40
Lowery, David, 24–25, 24n1

madness, 71–72, 85–86, 110–11, 115. See also unreason
materialize, 112–13
meaning, 14; lineages of, 66–67; meaninglessness, 59; as never fixed, 24–25, 33–34; speaking and, 31–32; of touch, 90; unmeaning, 20–21, 44, 49, 55; unreason and, 79–80, 112
mediation, 32, 38–39; touch and, 90–91. See also immediacy
meditation, 1, 23
melancholy, 15–16
memory, 13–14, 79–80, 83, 92–93, 98–101, 114, 125; of dismemberment, 18–19; intensify, 46–47; of one's life, 24, 26–28; as physical, 18; trauma and, 18–19
metaphor, 48–49, 57–58
Metis, 7n7, 32, 35–36, 44
middle voice, 2, 2n2, 7–8, 37n1, 66, 66n1
mind, 1–2, 7–10, 23, 57–58, 60–61, 63–65, 71–72, 74, 94, 101, 122; mindbody, 83–84
mindfulness, 3, 93–94
Monet, Claude, 75n9
moon, moonlight, 48–49, 53–54, 84, 99–102, 128–29
morality: bifurcating divisions of, 36, 67–68, 71–74, 107–8, 117; breaching, 72–73, 75–79; knowledge, reason, truth and, 36, 71–72, 107–8, 117; seriousness and, 59–61; unreason and, 74–75, 77–78; value of, 61–62
Moses, 46n1
movement, 17n1, 34–35, 46–47, 50–53, 62, 116–17
MS Berlin, 94–95
Mt. Horeb, 46n1
museum. See Guggenheim Museum

music, 24–25, 49–50, 52, 57–58, 94, 97–98. See also Dylan, Bob
mystery, 39–40, 46, 69–70, 74–76, 83, 129

Naas, Michael, 118–21, 123
names, naming, 8, 12, 24, 37n1, 51, 58, 60–61, 67, 73–74, 85–86, 106–7, 112–15, 118–19
narrative, 3, 110, 123. See also telling
Nietzsche, Friedrich, 57–58, 67n2, 75n9, 76, 76n10, 112–13; on attempters, 58–59, 67; experience of creation, 62–64; free spiritedness, 58–62, 64–65, 67, 75; gaiety of life, 61–62; influences, 64; on mentoring, 102–4; on truth, 59–63. See also riddles, riddlers
night, 8, 11, 26–28, 37, 39, 45, 47, 54–55, 71–72, 91–93, 95, 100–103, 128–29
noise, 1, 15–16, 29–30, 38, 51–53, 81–82, 90
nomads, nomadic, 12, 32–33, 50, 107; nomadic freedom, 69–71, 105–8, 112, 115, 117. See also exiles, exilic
nomós, 32–33. See also law
normalcy, normality, normativity, 32–33, 71; breaching, 76–68; outside, 85–86
North American Society for Philosophical Hermeneutics, 6, 6n6, 13n1
nothing, no thing, 9–10, 23, 26–28, 44, 82–84; airy, 85–88, 109–10, 112–13, 128–29; chaos and, 67; darkness and, 45; death and, 29–30, 92–93, 121–22; emptiness and, 55–56; feeling, 29, 92–93; gap of, 19; hearing, 37, 41–42; life and, 29–30, 119–20; meaning and, 15,

114–15; night's, 39; resolves, 18–19; silence and, 1, 5, 7–8, 37, 64–66, 66n1, 70–71, 78–80, 78n11, 81–82, 84, 99–101, 107, 112, 129; time and, 121, 123; true to, 21; unreason and, 72–78, 114–15, 117
noticing, 1, 43–44, 90n3

O'Keefe, Georgia, 53–56
objectification, objectivity, 109–10, 112n8; escaping, 58–59; ideal object, 7–8; language and, 4, 31–32; non-objectivity, 50n3, 53; rational, 113–15; silence and, 1, 6–9
ocean, 43–44, 46, 51, 81, 100–101, 103–4
Oceanus, 35–36
Oliver, Mary, 100
opposites, opposition, 41, 59–61, 67, 71–79, 112, 112n8; breaching, 67–68, 78–79, 105
order, 9–10; absence of, 57–58, 117; breaching, 72–75, 78–79; silence and, 20–22; trauma's interruptive gap, 19; wonder and, 86. *See also* chaos; unorder
outcast, 69–70, 74, 111–12. *See also* exile, exilic; leprosy; unreason

painting, 17–18, 17n1, 53–56, 71–72, 100. *See also* O'Keefe, Georgia; Vallega, Alejandro
palm at the end of the mind, 9–10
panic, 24–25, 71–72
Parmenidean Way, 51
pasture (*nomós*), 32–33
pathos, 17–18, 34
peace of mind, 5, 120–21
perception, 37–39, 47, 48–49, 54–56, 75. *See also* senses, sensing

performative, 11–12, 34, 59, 78n11; happenings, 11–12; of life death, 119
Peri Hermeneias (*De interpretatione*, Aristotle), 33
phenomenon, 31n1
philosophy, 3, 3n4, 19, 58–59, 75, 118; as border art, 35n3; postmodern, 76n10
phoenix, 9–10
Picasso, Pablo, 50–51, 50n2, 75n9
Pinochet, Augusto, 17–18, 18n2
Plato, 119–20
poetry, 3, 9–10, 20–21, 26–28, 34, 39–40, 48–49
poietic creation (*poiein*), 1, 3–4; airy nothing and, 85–86; as border art, 35; as dynamic, porous, often fluid, and uncertain, 3–4; as moment of transformation, 4; non-objectivity of, 53; poietic language, 3–4; poietic sensing and, 49; poietic thinking, 3 4
possibility, 19, 24–25, 41, 43, 49–50, 57–60, 63–64, 68–69, 79–80, 110–12, 128
power, 1, 4–5, 32–34, 51–55, 78–79, 84–85, 112n8; of freedom, 69–71; in gap, 19; of life itself, 119–23; of reason, 71–80, 105–8, 110–15, 112n8, 117; of silence, 15–16, 66, 103–4, 117; of truths, 59–61, 65
pre-reflective, 38, 43, 60–61, 66, 74, 89–91
presence: absence and, 18, 100; enabling, 55; gap in, 82–84; identity and, 4–5; indeterminate, 23–24; silent, 53–55, 82–84; time and, 14; uninterrupted, 1–2; vital, 15, 103–4. *See also* absence
Prognosticator, 24–25

PTSD (post-traumatic stress disorder), 82–83
purity, 51, 73, 105–7, 109–10, 120

race: racism and, 94–95; touching, 90, 94–95
reading, 4–5, 9–10, 11–12, 21, 34, 51–53, 60–65, 68–69, 86, 93, 118
real, reality, 12; breaches in, 67–68; as frightening, tenuous, nebulous, 49; imagined, 23–24, 107, 111–12, 123; of life itself, 120–21; obscured or ignored dimensions of, 75–76; silence and, 100, 119–20
really silent, 41–44
reason, rationality, 71–72; absence of, 111–12; authority of, 105–11, 112n8, 113–14, 117; breaching, 76–69; end of, 10; morality and, 107–8, 114; objectification and, 109–10, 112n8, 113–15; occurrences that happen as no thing, 66; secular, 107–8, 114; unsettling, 74–75, 75n9, 77–78. *See also* unreason
Rebay, Hilla. 50n3
recognition, 8, 18–19, 32–33, 66–68, 73–74, 77, 92–93
recuperation, 19
relation, 1–2, 6, 19, 63–64
release, 26–28, 44
repose, 29–30
reserve, 16, 103
reticence, 15–16, 103–4
reversal, 69–70, 78–79, 117, 121, 123
reversion, 119
rhododendrons, 97–99, 97n1
Richard, Nelly, 18, 18n2
riddles, riddlers, 58–62, 65, 67, 75–79. *See also* attempters; Nietzsche, Friedrich
Rilke, Rainer Maria, 112–13

Rivera, Diego, 75n9
Rivera, Omar, 13n1
Rock Ethics Institute (Penn State University), 125–26
Rousseau, Jean-Jacques, 75n9, 112–13
rupture, 18, 110–11

Sade, Marquis de, 112–13
sadness, 16, 26–28, 62, 126
Santayana, George, 75n9
Schelling, Friedrich W. J., 75n9
Schleiermacher, Friedrich, 34–35, 112–13
Schopenhauer, Arthur, 64
sea, 95, 100–104, 108–9. *See also* ocean
security, 23, 66–67, 81–82, 106–7
senses, sensing, 48–49; beyond, 10, 54–55; at boundary of what is speakable, 85–86; images of, 101–2; immediacy of, 11–14, 91–93; indefinite, 49; metaphor and, 48–49; poietic, 49; presence and, 53–54; silence and, 23, 31–32, 37–39, 49–56; unreason and, 71; vastness of, 13–14; world, 55
sensibilities, 43, 46–47; attuned to unreason, 76–77; lineages of, 74; for problems, 66–67; with silences, 43–44
seriousness, 60–64
Shakespeare, William: *A Midsummer Night's Dream*, 22, 85–86, 109–10; *The Tempest*, 95n6
shock, 4, 43–44, 82
shooting stars, 20
sight, seeing, 7–8, 31–32, 45–46, 90, 101–2. *See also* senses, sensing; visibility
silence: absence and, 70–71, 100, 110; as anomalous, 8–9; attunements to, 1–2; awareness of and in, 1,

5–6, 36–38, 43, 100; beauty of, 116–17; *in* bifurcating imagery of opposites, 67–68, 71; borders of, 35; boundaries if, 8; breaching, 73–74, 76–79; chaos and, 9; in coming of yet to come, 50; conceiving, 7–8; cultivating, 5; darkness and, 102; death and, 5–6, 41–42, 92–93, 121–22; devoted love and, 87; dignity of, 15; disorder and, 64–65; division and, 71–73; in exclusion and objectification, 114–15; experience of, 43–44, 53, 55–56; feeling with, 4, 9–10, 20–21, 38–40, 44, 83–84, 86, 97–98, 119–20; finding oneself-in-transition and, 50; as formed situation, 78; freedom and, 74–75, 106–7; as gap, 18–19, 35, 82–84; germinal, 19; happening of, 7–9, 11–12, 38, 46–47, 66, 78–79, 81–82, 87; haunting, 23–25; of home, 26–29, 98–99; images of, 5–6, 38, 67–68, 78–79, 81–82, 98 101, 115; imagining, 48–49; immediacy of, 2, 13–14, 41; in-between, 14; as incomprehensible, 47; indefinite, 58–61, 66–67; indeterminate, 39, 67; of indirection, 38; interpreting, 44; invisibility of, 18; lack of identity, 8–9; language appropriate to, 36; lightening burden of everyday life, 1–2; love and, 128–30; meaninglessness of, 9–10, 20–21, 44, 59; metaphor and, 48–49; music-not-yet, 50; non-objectivity of, 3, 5–9, 31–32, 35, 44; non-place of, 12, 64; as no thing, 23–24, 39, 41, 64–66, 83–84, 86; noticing, 1–2; objectless, 51; of ocean, 43–44; permeating bodies, 1–2; pervading spaces of sound, 1–2, 8–9, 100–101; power of, 15–16, 66, 103–4, 117; presence and, 53–54, 103–4; rupturing, 110–11; sensibilities with, 43; sensing, 23, 31–32, 38, 46–47, 49–53, 55–56; shining, 97; *in* silence, 1–4, 8, 48–49; silence silencing, 2–5, 7–12, 19–21, 29–30, 37–38, 37n1, 41, 44, 64–66, 75, 78–82, 78n11, 100; situated, 8; space of, 23, 54–55, 84–87, 117; speaking of, 37; of stars, 43–44; sticky, 8, 78–79, 78n11, 81; subjectless, 51; tantalizing, 9–10; telling, 1–4, 11–12, 20, 57; time and, 29–30, 58–59, 121; touch and, 89–96; trauma and, 82–83; of undetermined future, 58–59; of universe, 24–25; unreason and, 111–15, 117, in vastness of, 54, 95–96; well-timed for effect, 9; writing about non-interpretively (interpreting silence), 5–8, 31–34

silencesounds, 14

silent gap, 82–84

skintouchingskin, 88–90, 93–94

slipperiness, 35–36

smile, 39–40, 44

snow, 20

songs, 1–2, 9–10, 50, 57–58, 117. *See also* music

sounds: of everyday life, 51–53; pervasion of silence, 1–2, 14, 23, 37–38, 46–47, 81, 100–101; on silent borders, 35. *See also* noise; silence

space: absence and, 83–84; of airy nothing, 85–87; of creation, 85–86; determining, 32; empty, 55–56; end of, 9–10; life-spaces, 84–85, 87, 87; liminal, 65; of non-objectivity, 51; non-places, 12, 23, 49, 64, shapes in, 52; of silence, 23, 54–55, 84–87,

space *(continued)*
   117; spacing out, 51; undefined, 85–86; *unheimlich*, 84–85; vastness of, 29–30, 81–83, 97; of wandering, 32–33
speak, speaking: boundary of, 85–86; at end of mind, 9–10; one who will not, 8; of silences, 31–32, 37, 67–68; unsayable, 48–49
spring, 116–17
Stevens, Wallace, "Of Mere Being," 9–10, 9n9
stickiness, 8, 73, 78–79, 81. *See also under* silence
stillness, 8, 20, 23, 26–28, 41–42, 99
stories, 17–19, 33–35, 64; of death, 121–22; of silence, 3, 8; of unreason, 67–69, 77–78, 105–7, 110–13, 114, 117
storms, 52–53, 62–63, 78–79, 101–2
streets, 9, 99, 101–2, 111
Sturm und Drang movement, 112–13
subjects, subjectivity, 2, 7–9, 14, 50–51, 76–77, 91–92, 94, 112n8
subjection, 67, 73–74, 120–21
subjunctive, 7–8, 8n8
sublime, sublimity, 102–3
succubi, 111
suffering, 17–19, 29–30, 34, 49–50, 52–53, 65, 71–72, 106–7, 112, 121–22
sun, 10, 13–14, 22, 24–25, 29–30, 48–49, 84, 97–98, 100–101, 116–17, 128–29. *See also* light

tantalizing, 9–10
telling, 2; darkness and, 45; delight in, 34; as revealing, 11; silence, 3–4, 6–8, 11–12, 20–21, 57, 121–22; stories, 34–35, 67–68, 105–6, 121–22
testimony, 19

things, 75, 77–78, 110–12; care of, 26–28; "essential thing," 68–69; imagined, 49, 100; make sense of, 43, 49, 55; too many, 1, 98; memorial, 26–28, 62–63; as object, 6–8; silence and, 8–9, 23–24, 29–30, 44; thingliness, 35–36; time of, 26–28. *See also* nothing, no thing
Thoth, 33
thresholds, 7–8; as between-being, 18; without community, 18–19; without configurations, 19; of dying, 118–19; to ether-like non place, 12; of indeterminacy, 67–68, 76, 95; never-ending, 65; of possibility, 112; senseless, 73–74; site of, 66–67
thunder, 101–102. *See also* lightning; storms
Tiethys, 35–36
time, temporality: agency of, 121; destabilization of, 7–8; fell time, 122–23; future and, 3–4, 58–59, 95; of happening, 7–8; of life death, 119; Life Itself and, 120–21; of love, 129–30; meaning and, 20, 55; of Now, 20–21; of poietic creation, 3–4; presence and, 14; as progression, 121; release from logics of, 13–14; of silence, 1, 29–30, 58–59, 121; of things, 26–28; vastness of, 29–30
touch, touching: awareness of, 92–93; beyond identity, 94; immediacy of, 92–95; in-between, 94–95; mindfulness with, 93; nothing, 92–93; between people, 88–95, 88n1, 89n2; as pre-reflective, 91; race, 94–95; silence, 93–96; without violation, 90n3
transform, transformation, 4, 19, 35–36, 40, 51, 60–61, 66–67, 74–75,

86–87, 89n2, 95, 103–4, 118, 123, 129–30
trauma, 24–25, 82–84; of dismembered society, 18–19; embodied, 18; generative possibilities in gap of, 19; memory and, 18–19; pervaded by silence silencing, 19
treacherous mentor, 102–4
trembling, 12, 88–89, 117
truth: animation in embodied life of mind, 64; breaching, 76–77; as changeable, 61; divisions of, 71–72; draw of simplification, 60–61; fabrications and, 68–69; forced-truths, 69–60; loss of nascent immediacy, 63; unreason and, 74–75; untruth, 21, 59, 102, 118; value of, 61–62
Tuana, Nancy, 6, 93, 124–29
two lovers, 124–29

uncanniness, 4, 53–54, 92–93, 98–99. See also *Unheimlichkeit*
uncertainty, 3–4, 83, 86–87; pervasive, 12; value of, 36
unclenched determination, 44
understanding: as affective, 17–18, 53–54; instabilities of, 35–36; life and, 118; of metaphor, 48–49; reason and, 114; silence and, 5, 31–32, 38, 40, 44, 57; trauma and, 17–19; turning away from, 44
Unheimlichkeit (uncanniness), 84–85, 98–99
unification, 4–5, 66–67
universe, 5, 24–25, 29–30, 37, 49–50, 107, 111–12
unorder, 20–21, 49, 59, 64–65, 67–68, 71–74, 78–79, 111, 114–15
unreason, 67–73, 69n6, 76–79, 105–7, 106n2, 112n8; confinement and, 73–74; as contagion, 109–12, 114; creativity and, 112–13; domestication of, 108–10; happening of, 112–13, 117; as opening, 110–11; silent, 78–79, 111–15, 117; as transforming imaginary, 74–75

Vallega, Alejandro, 17–19, 17n1, 18n2
van Gogh, Vincent, 75n9
vastness: of desert, 53–56; of ocean, 43–44, 95, 103; of sensuous, 13–14; of silence, 33–34, 80, 81–83, 81n1, 85–87, 97; taciturnity, 102–4; of universe, 24–25, 29–30, 37, 95, 98
verge, 81–82, 81n2
violence, 34, 43, 73, 101–2; conception as, 7–8; as ever-present potential happening, 17–18, 44; of touch, 90n3
"Virginia's House," 26–28
visibility, 6–7, 31–32, 57. *See also* invisibility
vitality, 15–16, 29–30, 50, 60–61, 103–4, 116–17, 123
volatility, 4–5, 79, 120
Voltaire, 112–13
vulnerability, 55n4, 129–30

wandering, 32–33, 39
water-world, 94–96
wholes. *See* objectification, objectivity
wicked thoughts, 62–73
Wilko, 26–28
wisdom, 35–36, 60, 129
Wollstonecraft, Mary, 112–13
wonder, 46, 55, 65, 81–87, 98–99, 123
world: birthing of new, 1, 58–59, 116–17; body and, 52; chaos and, 57–58; of continuous change, 61–62; falsified, 59–61; logics of, 13, 67–68, 77–78, 94, 107, 111–13;

world *(continued)*
    make, 80; as mysterious, 39–40, 75; open to more, 12; sense of, 49, 55, 63–64, 68–69, 74, 89–90; silence and, 1–2, 4–5, 12, 20, 39, 44; as site of thresholds, 66–67; space of, 84–85; trauma and, 82–84; vastness of, 29–30; world-creations, 117; world-shift, 51

Wright, Frank Lloyd, 50–51

yet-to-be, 50. *See also* indeterminacy
Zeus, 32–35, 46n1

www.ingramcontent.com/pod-product-compliance
Lightning Source LLC
Chambersburg PA
CBHW030828230426
43667CB00008B/1430